Cambridge Elements ☰

Elements in Contentious Politics
edited by
David S. Meyer
University of California, Irvine
Suzanne Staggenborg
University of Pittsburgh

T0311520

HAVE REPERTOIRE, WILL TRAVEL

Nonviolence as Global Contentious Performance

Selina R. Gallo-Cruz
Syracuse University

CAMBRIDGE
UNIVERSITY PRESS

CAMBRIDGE
UNIVERSITY PRESS

Shaftesbury Road, Cambridge CB2 8EA, United Kingdom

One Liberty Plaza, 20th Floor, New York, NY 10006, USA

477 Williamstown Road, Port Melbourne, VIC 3207, Australia

314–321, 3rd Floor, Plot 3, Splendor Forum, Jasola District Centre,
New Delhi – 110025, India

103 Penang Road, #05–06/07, Visioncrest Commercial, Singapore 238467

Cambridge University Press is part of Cambridge University Press & Assessment,
a department of the University of Cambridge.

We share the University's mission to contribute to society through the pursuit of
education, learning and research at the highest international levels of excellence.

www.cambridge.org
Information on this title: www.cambridge.org/9781009484008

DOI: 10.1017/9781009484015

First published 2024

A catalogue record for this publication is available from the British Library.

ISBN 978-1-009-48400-8 Hardback
ISBN 978-1-009-48398-8 Paperback
ISSN 2633-3570 (online)
ISSN 2633-3562 (print)

Have Repertoire, Will Travel

Nonviolence as Global Contentious Performance

Elements in Contentious Politics

DOI: 10.1017/9781009484015
First published online: February 2024

Selina R. Gallo-Cruz
Syracuse University

Author for correspondence: Selina R. Gallo-Cruz, srgalloc@syr.edu

Abstract: Nonviolence is celebrated and practiced around the world, as a universal "method for all human conflict." This Element describes how nonviolence has evolved into a global repertoire, a patterned form of contentious political performance that has spread as an international movement of movements, systematizing and institutionalizing particular forms of protest as best claims-making practice. It explains how the formal organizational efforts of social movement emissaries and favorable and corresponding global models of state and civic participation have enabled the globalization of nonviolence. The Element discusses a historical perspective of this process to illuminate how understanding nonviolence as a contentious performance can explain the repertoire's successes and failures across contexts and over time. The Element underscores the dynamics of contention among global repertoires and suggests future research more closely examine the challenges posed by institutionalization.

Keywords: collective action repertoire, contentious performances, nonviolence, globalization, world polity

ISBNs: 9781009484008 (HB), 9781009483988 (PB), 9781009484015 (OC)
ISSNs: 2633-3570 (online), 2633-3562 (print)

Contents

Introduction

One way to think about the globalization of nonviolence is to consider a sample of global news events that occurred during the drafting of this manuscript.

In 2021, following news of the military coup in Myanmar, a proclamation was issued on the United States Institute of Peace (USIP) webpage in support of the country's elected government, led by renowned Burmese nonviolent leader Aung San Suu Kyi:

> The people of Myanmar have opposed military rule in the past but never like this: In the face of horrific brutality by a lawless regime, Burmese have risen up in an historic national movement of nonviolent resistance. Led by young women, the fractious country has united across ethnic, generational and class lines, weaponizing social norms and social media in a refusal to accept the generals' February 1 seizure of power.
>
> (Oo, Ford, and Pinckney 2021)

A chorus of peace scholars and pundits joined the USIP in rallying behind the Burmese movement, praising not only its noble resistance against an unjust coup but also expressing faith in the use of nonviolence to carry the movement to democracy (Oo, Ford, and Pinckney 2021). Sadly, since this initial outpouring of support, the military junta has killed over fifteen hundred civilian resisters.

Meanwhile, advocates in the Middle East called for nonviolence to be employed in Afghanistan in opposition to the oppressive tactics of the Taliban (McCarthy 2021) and for Jewish allies to bolster the noncooperative power of Palestinian activists through nonviolent solidarity (Amro and Witus 2021). A history of violence has long defined both of these political fields. Similarly, Indigenous forest-dwelling peoples in the Brazilian Amazon regularly face violence at the hands of extractive logging and mining industries. Although some Indigenous monitors are armed for self-defense – an approach made necessary by reports that Indigenous leaders in Brazil are being murdered at the highest rate in over two decades (Hanbury 2019) – nonviolence is an important part of their work as well (Gómez-Upegui 2021). Finally, in 2022, peace scholars rushed in to defend the legitimacy of nonviolence in the face of the Russian invasion of Ukraine. This required advocates to navigate a tangled web of geopolitical alliances and economic interests in the region, in addition to a resurgence of Cold War animosities. Still, they have persisted in encouraging greater support for nonviolent civilian resistance to the military offensive in Ukraine and Russia (Christoyannopoulos 2022; Hunter 2022).

These examples point to a paradox for scholars of global contentious politics: despite a long, dynamic history of global nonviolence and an impressive global industry for nonviolent movement training and support, old tensions continue to morph into new, seemingly unceasing violent conflicts. Nonetheless, those dedicated to nonviolence as the best form of claims-making and resistance believe nonviolence to be an appropriate response to even the most dire of violent conflicts. This raises questions about how and why nonviolence has spread so successfully to be recognized as the best form for democratic claims-making. In this study, I explore why nonviolence has been celebrated as a global repertoire across distinct conflicts in contexts characterized by starkly inequitable power dynamics and complex histories of repressive violence.

There is one kind of story that has become common in the scholarship on nonviolent resistance and civil resistance studies, which have grown substantially in the decades since I first began this research.[1] Although this narrative might be imparted implicitly, it describes a family of protest techniques that have emerged organically. This emergence was helped along by some big names who publicized and shared their knowledge of nonviolent techniques, as well as the concatenation of thousands upon thousands of individual instances in which nonviolent resistance was performed and perfected because in each of those instances it made sense to employ it as "a force more powerful" in line with unarmed resisters' goals of democracy and peacemaking. This story is not wholly untrue, but it is patently incomplete and makes understanding the follow-up questions of how and why nonviolence can be effective difficult to answer fully.

As I explain below, nonviolence has become a global movement of movements conceptualizing, systematizing, and institutionalizing nonviolent protest as best practice for democratic state-making on a global scale. This movement is embedded in a contemporary cultural and political world order that has shaped and enabled its spread while it has in turn been shaped by the diffusion of nonviolence. Thus, this global historical perspective allows for a new understanding of when and how nonviolent movements work. While it may be useful to strategists to examine each unique nonviolent movement as a particular case in a particular context in order to understand the strategic action dynamics of distinct outcomes, a global perspective on how nonviolence came to be

---

[1] In his introduction to the history of civil resistance studies, Timothy Ash explains that the concept of "civil resistance" denotes one type of nonviolent action that has increased in popular use because it encompasses the key qualities of many case studies of interest: a civic action involving advocacy for a broad level of social change; the employment of normative resistance against targets, though not necessarily disobedience; and avoidance of violent means, though not necessarily as a result of a strong philosophical commitment to nonviolence (Ash 2009; see also Randle 1994; Stiehm 1968). I use the term nonviolence in my work to include both explicit engagement with nonviolence as resistance, sometimes coupled with an exploration of nonviolence as a way of life, and the many forms of nonviolent action that the movement to globalize nonviolence has helped to spread, popularize, and institutionalize as best practice through both the formal and informal dissemination of knowledge.

understood, practiced, spread, and celebrated can shed new light on why movements have increasingly adopted nonviolent techniques and why their practice of nonviolence has generated different results in different political contexts and at different points in geopolitical time. Furthermore, I argue that a global understanding of nonviolence as a movement of movements illuminates some of strategic action scholarship's blind spots in ways that will be crucial for making sense of contemporary conflicts and shifts in geopolitical power.

Take again the examples of the conflicts presented above. Can you imagine a different historical and geopolitical context in which those in power in Myanmar, Israel/Palestine, Afghanistan, the Brazilian Amazon, or Ukraine might respond more effectively to nonviolent civil resistance? What if those regimes and powerholders were already at the precipice of a retreat from power, such as at the end of the Eastern Bloc? What if they could be shamed by political allies who threatened to withdraw their economic support? What if the forms of governance or change that the nonviolent resisters proposed offered greater benefit to actors seeking legitimacy and inclusion in their political landscape? With these questions in mind, I think it is easier to understand how nonviolence would and could work well in these conflicts, as it has before in similar situations. A big picture understanding, however, requires a global historical analysis, a macro level of analysis that has been elided in the case study focus of many studies of nonviolent movements.

Overview

In the pages to follow, I provide a global and historical study of how nonviolence emerged as a contentious performance among claims-makers the world over. After briefly reviewing the literature on contentious political forms and discussing my data and methods, I present a global, cultural, and historical study of nonviolence in three sections. First, I trace the global history of nonviolence through four distinct waves of globalization. The first phase is early conceptualization, when formative figures developed the foundational ideas and models that came to be carried into new conflicts around the world. The second phase is the subsequent era of systematization, during which the field of research dedicated to understanding nonviolence as a general practice took off and new influential actors and organizations devised formal and systematic ways of sharing those skills and knowledge. The third and fourth phases unfolded in the later half of the twentieth century, when the organizational field for global nonviolence proliferated rapidly and movements developed innovative local expressions of nonviolent practices. Here, I detail the many ways in which established global civic and political network increased the influence of the nonviolent repertoire.

This history demonstrates that nonviolence did not emerge spontaneously or organically as some with faith in the natural superiority of nonviolent methods might assume. Rather, it reveals the complex efforts of an intentional community of activists dedicated to developing nonviolence as a global cultural and political practice.

I provide a behind the scenes understanding of nonviolence organizations as a dynamic social force in the story of how unique movement actors, the forms of authority they wield, and the resources they mobilize can shape the way citizens protest in some of the most contentious conflicts around the world.

In a second section, I dig deeper into how and why nonviolence has emerged against the backdrop of significant changes in the world polity over the long twentieth century. This allows me to elaborate on nonviolence as a global contentious repertoire, developed iteratively in response to changes in their corresponding governments. My research both confirms and builds upon Tilly's insights into the development of cultural content for the nonviolence repertoire as a significant social force shaping diffusion, institutionalization, and ultimately contentious performances of collective action. I also explain here why this global and cultural perspective is invaluable to understanding how nonviolence works and when it does not.

Finally, I discuss an oversight that demands new attention if we are to better understand what modern movements are up against today: the institutional paradoxes posed by predictability and systematization. These features have been shown to have many benefits for movements' development, but they also often spell the end of success and innovation rendering movements vulnerable to cooptation and demobilization. In an age where public relations and market and politically oriented maneuvers have all but supplanted journalistic inquiry and democratic engagement, I suggest scholars of nonviolent movements and those interested in movement strategies and tactics across borders give far greater attention to how nonviolence's long history of successes as a global claims-making repertoire has created new opportunities for the appropriation of people-power.

A summary of distinct claims developed in this Element is listed on page 39–40.

Audiences

I have written this work with several audiences in mind. This project began as a way of recording my observations about activists working to formalize and carry nonviolent techniques around the world, which piqued my interest in the larger nonviolence network. I have learned much from those doing the global work of nonviolence and I hope they will learn something from the detailed historical work I have done here.

For scholars of nonviolent movements, this study takes quite a different tack than the normative orientation in the field. Unlike much of this work, I do not position my study at the level of the psychology of individual protesters who choose nonviolent techniques nor do I present a psychological analysis of how individuals engage within transnational nonviolent networks (although elsewhere I have examined how nonviolent NGOs work among grassroots organizers). Rather, I take a global and cultural approach to understanding the repertoire's development over time. I present an in-depth investigation into how nonviolence has emerged and become so firmly established as best claims-making practice for citizens around the world. Through this analytic process, I arrive at new insights into the effects of nonviolence's global institutionalization that help to explain how and why nonviolence sometimes works well and at other times fails those who use it.

Throughout the development of this research, I have been firmly committed to understanding the process of repertoire emergence outlined by Tilly. Here I contribute new understanding to the nature of contentious performances and repertoire emergence on a global scale through the deeply cultural processes of meaning-making and structuration.

To world society and globalization theories, and world polity theory in particular, I offer new conclusions about the role and consequences of claims-making repertoires as driven by tactical movements. I believe this theoretical tradition is uniquely well-positioned to generate valuable knowledge about the threat institutionalization poses to social movements by encouraging more critical thinking about the nature of power in the face of unique opportunities for movement capture, cooptation, and demobilization.

Collective Action Repertoires as Contentious Performances

There are two possibilities when one attends a musical performance. The audience may expect a group of musicians to play a collection from a particular genre and style of music, whether because the audience is familiar with the group, the group is playing in a particular venue known for featuring a particular kind of music, or the show was billed as such. However, it is also always possible the musicians will play a different kind of music by bending and extending styles or by playing a different genre altogether. Musical repertoires may be unique to different musicians and groups, but they are also collectively developed, shared, learned, and celebrated over time. While there are many different possible repertoires musicians can develop, they often reflect certain patterns, allowing many different groups to develop the same or very similar repertoires within and across musical genres that can broadly endure for a very long time. For all of these reasons, historical and political sociologist Charles Tilly applied a similar perspective to the study of contentious politics introducing the concept of a "collective action repertoire." This term for contentious performances that consist of "limited set[s] of routines that are learned, shared, and acted out" (Tilly 1993, 264) provides an apt imagery for describing claims-making patterns around which social movements often cohere.

As Tilly explained in his work on claims-making repertoires, the possibilities for contentious action are "learned through struggle." Each commonly known act of political protest has an origin story related to a particular contention, a particular political and cultural context, and even the technological environment in which actors were situated. However, Tilly added, despite these possibilities, claims-making routines are also limited in practice: "At any point in history, however, [people] learn only a rather small number of alternative ways to act collectively" (Tilly 1993, 264).

In order to understand these claims-making routines, it is important to consider how and under what conditions they become institutionalized as the predominant repertoires drawn on by resisters. Tilly devised the concept and framework for understanding claims-making repertoires as "contentious performances" in his studies of protest and state formation. Scouring archival records of political contention in eighteenth century France, Tilly observed a phenomenal shift in how people organized their protests against authorities. Broadening his study of contention to Great Britain around the same time, he also found that this shift occurred with the crystallization of new forms of governance in Western Europe. New repertoires of political contention, he concluded, evolved as new kinds of polities took shape. In these cases, the emergence of national governments organized around parliamentary politics was followed by transformations from formerly local-level acts of resistance toward nationally organized campaigns. Once unique expressions of discontent, like food riots in response to price gouging or the breaking down of enclosures to protest the division of common lands relied upon by locals, were replaced by modular techniques able to serve many different localities, actors, and issues. And, as former subjects evolved into entitled citizens, the "parochial, particular, and bifurcated eighteenth-century repertoire" soon gave way to more autonomous claims made on the resisters' own initiative (Tilly 1993). Further, many of the new, historically unique forms Tilly documented as emerging at this crucial juncture – the rally, the strike, the march, and the boycott, among others – would later become central to the nonviolence repertoire. These repertoires then became institutionalized, in turn constraining the array of routines resisters would draw on in the centuries to come.

Since Tilly first introduced these ideas, scholars have extended and applied them into different national case studies. Tilly's assertions about repertoire emergence and institutionalization have been affirmed and elaborated upon through studies of El Salvador, France, Guatemala, Italy, Japan, and the United States, for example (Traugott 1995). This research suggests that social relations, meanings, and actions cluster in known, recurrent patterns and that resistance is shaped by the national political context in which they develop. In each of these cases, claims-making repertoires were also found to adhere to a modern, transposable form uniquely reflecting local "moral economies" that help to conceptualize and legitimate claims, forming the "tactical grammar" around which resisters unite (Ennis 1987).

To be clear, this scholarship has not shown strategic thinking to be insignificant. Rather, good strategies are found to emerge from the social world as scripts that actors can employ in the theater of resistance. Repertoires become important strategic organizational devices because movements commit to them and repertoires in turn influence movement communities in ways that parallel how movements influence national polities. Repertoires shape the path of social movements. They open up spaces of contention over the meanings, goals, and identities that activists share and spread with replicable consequences (McCammon 2003; Taylor et al. 2009). Indeed, repertoires help compel movements to "spillover" into other movements (Meyer and Whittier 1994), even if they become fragmented (Wada 2012), are mediated by existing social systems of stratification (Beckfield 2010; Feree and Merrill 2000) or become hybridized by the contingencies of the conflict at hand (Mueller 1999). To further extend the imagery of a musical routine, repertoires define the mood and the meaning of the protest. This is quite different than assuming actors choose repertoires from a free-floating array of options. Instead, movements have come to understand that protests should be organized in a particular way in order to be effective.

Tilly later argued that this now institutionalized repertoire helped to spread a general international understanding of social movements: "In advance of the social movement's institutionalization, the demonstration itself is spreading well beyond democratic regimes as a means of challenging corrupt and authoritarian rulers" (2006, 205). Scholars focused on the nexus between movements and formal politics have found that movements are defined by their social positionality as working outside of formal politics (although not always exclusively) and by their endurance in a political field as non-state actors that issue sustained challenges to powerholders (Tilly and Tarrow 2007). At the same time, they also fold into an overlapping field of contentious politics that includes movement tactics and formal political challenges (Ray 1999). Movements work themselves into this broader political field in distinct but overlapping ways (see Ray 1999),[2] operating as a force that gives rise to new political parties, courts, legislatures, and elections, and bridges institutionalized and noninstitutionalized politics in Western democracies, non-Western democracies and, in an increasingly globalized world, the variety of hybrid and autocratic regimes where social movements have played a role (Goldstone 2003; McCammon and Banaszak 2018; Rucht and Neidhardt 2002).

Tilly later lamented that more had not been done in the field to examine the development of the claims-making repertoire. He wished for greater verification, modification, or falsification of his ideas, acknowledging the limitations of the geographical areas and time periods in which he first devised the concept. In *Contentious Performances*, Tilly (2008) undertook his own extension and exploration of his repertoire emergence thesis by surveying research on the breakdown of the Soviet Union and the "tide of nationalist claims" that erupted from 1987 to 1992 (Beissinger 2002) in Mexico (drawing on work by Tamayo 1999), Italy, and the United States, and by taking a new look at events in Great Britain and France. Through this work, he explored how changes in the repertoire unfolded and he expanded the typology of repertoires. Still, he found that changes in how people protested made claims-making repertoires stronger and more enduring as they continued to be organized under a broader family of contentious performances. Although one of the principal objectives of this follow-up study was to ask "how different sorts of performance, including social movement performances, vary and change" (7), he ultimately concludes that "overwhelmingly, public collective contention involves strong repertoires. It involves collective learning and incessant adaptation" (15).

Although Tilly's (2008) illuminating reassessment involved broadly expanded analyses, each was nationally organized and much remains to be understood about the discursive and organizational dimensions of learning and adaptation. Here, I expand the framework of repertoire emergence analysis with a global study of the development and spread of nonviolence. As I also focus on the cultural and organizational dimensions of repertoire development and diffusion, my approach is distinct from earlier nationally organized repertoire emergence studies in a number of ways.

---

[2] Ray's field theoretical approach to social movements offers another useful theoretical framework for thinking about the emergence of repertoires on a global scale, across distinct national contexts and through the concepts outlined by Bourdieu in field theory. I offer field analysis in other works on nonviolence's globalization in Gallo-Cruz (2016b) and Gallo-Cruz (2021b).

First, instead of focusing on the clustering of groups of nonviolent action techniques, I examine the ways in which nonviolence (which includes the secular and neoliberal concept of "nonviolent civil resistance" or "civil resistance") has been culturally construed and socially institutionalized. As I will explain below, my research demonstrates how this family of tactics has become bundled conceptually and in practice through the development of formally organized protest training programs with certain philosophical moral understandings and commitments.

Second, unlike examining national studies in distinct time periods, a global historical survey of nonviolence allows for both comparative and systemic understanding. I follow the development of the repertoire in concept and practice over the long twentieth century. This allows me to compare how nonviolence has spread and been implemented in different political and cultural contexts and at different historical junctures.

Finally, as the thesis in the book's title suggests, the spread of this repertoire involves a story of formal diffusion and informal adoption that is common to the globalization of political structures and norms. Contrary to misguided criticism arguing that global institutional theories erase the agency of the actors, I trace the repertoire development work of actors who have invested their lives and resources into building a global nonviolence network. I examine how the understanding of global nonviolence as best practice for claims-making in "civil societies" has been formed and promoted, and the ways in which these ideas have been coupled with other political forms favorable to Western and neoliberal ideas of democracy. This grand effort includes the now expansive work of scholars celebrating the repertoire through the growing field of nonviolent studies, which experienced a surge in both private funding and academic attention as I began this project over a decade ago. As I seek to include the development of this field in my analysis, in this sense, I present a sociology of knowledge of nonviolent studies that sheds new light on some of the common assumptions about nonviolence and "nonviolent civil resistance."

A Global Approach to Repertoire Emergence

There are three elements of the repertoire emergence framework that I find essential to understanding the globalization of nonviolence. The first is the assertion of an iterative causal relationship between social movement forms and polity formation at the core of Tilly's (1993) repertoire emergence thesis. As Tilly noted in his study of early European state formation, this process has drawn on Western liberal ideals of democracy, a point also underscored in the extensive scholarship on world polity theory (Meyer et al. 1997). Second, it has been documented that national social movement repertoires become institution-alized and increasingly predictable over time, though some incremental innov-ation continues to occur at the margins (Tilly 1993). A global perspective on repertoires has significant implications for how political forms too easily become decoupled in practice (Clark 2010; Jupille et al. 2013; Koenig 2008; Swiss 2009), and in this case, helps to explain the diversity of forms and interpret-ations as well as the unevenness of repertoire success on a global scale. Finally, I will both address growing concerns over endogeneity in the formal study of nonviolent movements (Anisin 2020; Case 2021; Lehoucq 2016; Scheurman 2022) while also making the case that broader insights into the inclination toward institutionalization are especially important to understanding the glo-balization of nonviolence especially because the element of surprise is intrin-sically linked to the success of these actions (Gregg 1935; Sharp 1970).

Globalization involves complex transformations in the structure of world society and can be defined as comprising of at least four elements: diffusion, the global spread of people, practices, and ideas; organization, the development of formal institutions, rules, and practices across borders; the increased inter-dependence of people, places, and markets; and a growing culture and con-sciousness of the world as one place (Lechner 2009, 15). In Robertson's (1992) early and foundational conceptualization of globalization, the element of cul-ture and consciousness was crucial. He defined globalization as "the compres-sion of the world and the intensification of consciousness of the world as a whole" (8). I will argue in the pages to follow that these frameworks are helpful to understanding the globalization of nonviolence as so much of its spread has occurred through the work of shaping consciousness around why nonviolence is best practice for democratic claims-making, whether the reason-ing is derived from philosophical or secular, strategic commitments.

Social movements are sometimes vital to the process of globalization. Movements constitute a "third force," alongside traditional political and eco-nomic actors, that shapes the global agenda and institutional infrastructure for international and domestic politics (Florini 2000; Boli and Thomas 1999). Movements act as authorities that formulate a general, universalist global agenda for social change (Berkovitch 1999; Boyle 2006; Hironaka 2014; Longhofer et al. 2016; Merry and Levitt 2017). Global movements spread cultural ideals across states to influence efforts as diverse as expanding women's rights and educational opportunities (Berkovitch and Bradley 1999; Ramirez and McEneany 1997; Suarez and Bromley 2012), the legalization of same-sex marriage and other protections related to sexual orientation (Frank and McEneany 1999), and environmental protections (Frank, Longhofer, and Schofer 2007).

INGOs are often central actors in global movements (Boli and Thomas 1997) and can serve as brokers that weave together global and local political fields (Bromley, Schofer, and Longhofer 2018; Cole and Perrier 2019; Gallo-Cruz 2016b; Merry 2006). Tarrow (2001) noted that INGOs participate in local mobilization by facilitating connections that lead to the creation of new political identities. This can be done through certification, which recognizes existing actors and processes; modeling, which assists with the adoption of norms and forms of collective action; and institutional appropriation, which makes an international institution's resources or affiliations available to local groups. Other scholars have demonstrated how transnational networks can help expand access to the new strategic opportunities that may arise from shifting global political norms (Barrett and Kurzman 2004; Tsutsui 2018). Movement diffusion through organizations also involves ontological tasks, which construe actors as worthy of specific rights (Gallo-Cruz 2016b).

Close study of particularly influential global organizations reveals the internal culture and politics that shape their advocacy work and how they approach barriers to those efforts (Hemment 2007; Watanabe 2019). Assessments of INGOs have found that their collective impact is just as important as their unique organizational legacies. Together, INGO communities create a "bee swarm" of movement consciousness and mobilizing opportunities, lending momentum to movements around the world (Hironaka 2014). Nonviolent studies' increased focus on global social movements has contributed to a better understanding of how globalization influences what might otherwise be considered "bottom up" processes of globally interconnected civil societies (Gallo-Cruz 2016c; Gallo-Cruz 2019).

Many global social movement studies focus on transformations in policy and politics. One line of world society research organized under the term "world polity theory" specializes in tracing the link between organizational ties and policy adoption (see Cole 2017). In comparing how this process works on a global scale, it is important to note that the world polity is different from a national polity in two important respects. The world polity has no centralized government (although the United Nations serves as a forum for intergovernmental dialogue and voluntary policy enactment) and no singular military force (although, again, both the UN peacekeeping forces and regional alliances like the North Atlantic Treaty Organization often act in a transnational capacity). For this reason, convergence and authority occur across and sometimes through the obstacles of contention and fragmentation (Beckfield 2003). As world polity research has shown how the structure and form of world politics experienced a dynamic wave of "isomorphism" through which global political agendas and norms became increasingly similar over the latter half of the twentieth century

(Meyer et al. 1997), I argue that world polity theory also serves as a useful lens through which to discuss contentious performances on a global level.[3]

Decades of research on the development of a world polity (see Krücken and Drori 2009) elaborate the theory's core thesis that "Many features of the contemporary nation-state derive from worldwide models constructed and propagated through global cultural and associational processes" (Meyer et al. 1997, 144–145). As Meyer and colleagues go on to explain, worldwide models define and legitimate agendas for local action. This shapes the structures and policies of nation-states and other national and local actors in virtually every domain of rationalized social life, including business, politics, education, medicine, science, and even the family and religion. These global cultural processes remain highly influential despite "structural isomorphism in the face of enormous differences in resources and traditions, ritualized and rather loosely coupled organizational efforts, and elaborate structuration to serve purposes that are largely of exogenous origins" (Meyer et al. 1997, 145).

Together, international organizations and their supporting social movements create "epistemic communities" that articulate what social problems the global community should address, as well as why and how to do so (Alasuutari and Qadir 2019; Boli and Thomas 1999). In doing so, INGOs and social movements work together to raise global consciousness, establish global authority, and formulate doctrines and policies that states and non-state actors alike are expected to adhere to as members of a world society (Boli and Thomas 1999).

World polity theory also makes the assertion that some global problems existed long before movements emerged to address them, akin to the political process tradition that Tilly contributed to (see Giugni 2009). It is therefore important to understand how the development of a world polity, and the proliferation of certain cultural ideals in the postwar era contributed to the origin of these movements (Boli and Thomas 1999). This period was characterized by an intensification of sociocultural and political models for globally authoritative organizations that could establish an international forum for policy, security, and development of all kinds (Meyer et al. 1997). The development of a global political agenda also unfurled through widescale decolonization. The global wave of decolonization strengthened the model of independent nation-states that has come to constitute a core feature of the world polity today, giving rise to new global opportunities for claims-making, especially as decolonization occurred in an uneven fashion due to the poverty, inequality, and economic precarity created by former colonial powers (Chase-Dunn 1999; Rist 2019).

---

[3] In fact, world polity theory in its early stages was in part inspired by Tilly's polity formation studies (Boli, Gallo-Cruz, and Mathias 2011).

The contentious politics framework and world society theory make many common and distinct assertions. Both emphasize the importance of how movements draw on scripts for action and models for change. Both areas of scholarship find that the nature of these scripts leaves little room for innovation, while acknowledging incremental change at the margins. Finally, these frameworks position the polity as a central organizing structure around which both formal political action and citizen resistance develop and have therefore found the relationship between action forms and governance structures to be significant and iterative.

They diverge in part according to methodological approaches. Contentious politics studies have relied primarily on national case analysis and large event count data collected over time. World polity theory also draws heavily from historical event data but is fundamentally transnational in its scope. This global orientation has led to a greater emphasis on the mechanics of how common models for action spread across localities. World polity theory is also strongly cultural in its close examination of discourse, the nature of legitimacy and authority, and transformations in norms and values as well as in tracing the historical decoupling of implementation.

I argue below that Tilly's framework helps to explain how particular collective action forms may be spread through the strengthening of favorable political structures, even as repertoires become more open to incremental innovations while navigating political contexts. I also explain below how the world polity thesis that political models become infused with legitimacy and access to global networks holds true in the globalization of nonviolence. A globalization framework helps to elucidate the nature of cultural construction and organizational diffusion as this process unfolds on a global scale. It also holds that related predictions on the decoupling between the adoption of a practice and practical implementation apply to nonviolence as well.

Detecting Global Repertoires

In "How to Detect and Describe Performances and Repertoires," Tilly (2008) notes that the study of repertoire emergence and transformation involves both a classified counts technique of computing frequencies of events in large catalogs of episodic data and a broad interpretive qualitative assessment of the kinds of events that transpired in a given period and how and under what conditions they began to change. To explore the factors that have shaped the globalization of nonviolence and to better understand the impact of that globalization, I have employed global comparative historical methods (Drori 2008). These have involved both count measures signaling the expansion of the nonviolence repertoire and an in-depth qualitative investigation into the conceptualization and institutionalization of non-violence among global claims-making networks.

My study began with constructing and comparing various historical records of nonviolent events as they unfolded over time in different eras and in relation to other events. This included a chronological count of the development of nonviolence in newspaper and print discourse, of major movements that drew explicitly on the nonviolent repertoire, of the founding of organizations explicitly dedicated to spreading nonviolence, and of other measures of nonviolence's spread and institutionalization such as global programs, educational programs, and awards. I drew data for this timeline from secondary and primary sources, including case studies of nonviolent movements from dozens of books and academic journal articles, which I then cross-referenced with campaign databases (Chenoweth 2019; Chenoweth and Lewis 2013; Chenoweth, Pinkney, and Lewis 2019; Swarthmore 2022). As opposed to the conventional approach in political science studies that measures only discrete campaigns, my analysis also took a broader historical look at movements that involved multiple campaigns, some lasting decades. This is important for understanding how the repertoire developed over the lifetime of various movements (see Tilly 2004).

For quantitative analyses of the organizational spread of nonviolence, I created a database of INGOs that are explicitly dedicated to diffusing and implementing nonviolent strategies for social and political conflict resolution. Demographic data on this population was drawn from the Union of International Associations' (UIA) annual *Yearbook of International Organizations*.[4] This database includes INGOs active in the global nonviolence network. I chose to exclude organizations whose only participation in nonviolence was to foster awareness of philosophical or religious orientations to nonviolence (e.g. "nonviolence as a way of life") without actively supporting nonviolent resistance movements. This yielded 211 organizations (Gallo-Cruz 2019). In prior studies focused specifically on the role of these global organizations, I have conducted qualitative analyses of what

---

[4] The UIA annual yearbook was initiated in 1907 by Henri La Fontaine and Paul Otlet with the goal of constructing "a master bibliography of the world's accumulated knowledge." According to the UIA, its annual *Yearbook of International Organizations* is "the world's oldest, largest and most comprehensive source of information on global civil society" (2012). The electronic database historically catalogs information from over 40,000 organizations. Information remains in the archive even after an organization dissolves. It is a central networking catalog for international organizations and most active INGOs (and intergovernmental organizations) regularly submit their information to be stored in this database. The UIA also frequently solicits data. The data submitted is voluntary, however, and the extent and breadth of data on any one organization can vary. The electronic database organizes data into a number of categories for which organizations can submit information. These include founding, history, aims and objectives, structure, languages spoken, secretariat, finance, IGO relations, NGO relations, activities, publications, and the countries in which the organization has members.

nonviolent INGOs do, how they specialize, and how specialization has developed, in addition to statistical analyses of their diffusion through different historical phases, regions, and issues (Gallo-Cruz 2012, 2019).

To trace the global growth of nonviolence in popular discourse, I drew data from ProQuest News, an international news archive, from 1911 to 2013. I conducted a search to measure the growth of English-language books published on the topic of nonviolence through the global Books in Print database.[5] I have supplemented this with rich content on the development and nature of the repertoire derived from various other sources, including online archives, reports from nonviolent organizations and networks, historical documents collected from the archives of Peace Brigades International (PBI) at McMaster University's Peace Archives, and my field work with Nonviolence International at their Washington, DC office. Tactical manuals and conference reports collected from Nonviolence International and the International Fellowship for Reconciliation and in-depth qualitative interviews also provided insight into the social world of global nonviolence organizations.[6] Interviews were conducted with organizers from PBI, Nonviolence International (including NI United States, NI Southeast Asia, NI Russia and New Independent States, and NI Latin America), Christian Peacemaker Teams (whose name has since changed to Community Peacemaker Teams), Witness for Peace, the International Center for Nonviolent Conflict, the International Fellowship for Reconciliation, Training for Change, and the War Resisters League to gain insight into their global strategies. These interviews provided me a behind-the-scenes understanding of the development of strategic campaigns, networks, and the field of nonviolent studies, as well as discourse, training, and issues related to translation, solidarity, and transnational support for various movements and regions. They also provided a window into the lives of some of the most influential scholars and practitioners of global nonviolence.

I also examined the timeline of major geopolitical events that resulted in structural shifts in the nature of the world polity. This timeline spanned from early conflicts over colonization through the World War II era, decolonization, the rapid proliferation of independent states in an international state system, the expansion of a global international organizational regime, the rise and fall of the Cold War, the development of modern civil wars, the development and diffusion of the arms industry, and a host of international agreements pertaining to peace, conflict, and international war. Drawing on data provided by the Banks Cross-National Time Series database (2009) and the Polity IV database (Gurr et al. 2010), I examined the global growth of violent conflicts and political change.

---

[5] Although this source includes only five English-speaking countries: the United States, the United Kingdom, Canada, Australia, and New Zealand.

[6] Beer (2021) of Nonviolence International has since published an anthology of these manuals.

This allowed me to weigh the global spread of nonviolence and the emergence of nonviolent movements against the development of democratic governance and autocratic repression. I considered the development of other violent resistance movements as well as the spread of civilian movements' access to arms.

Below, I first describe the globalization of nonviolence chronologically, beginning with its early conceptualization as a universal strategic action repertoire before moving into an examination of its formal application to global conflicts by major actors. In line with Lechner's (2009) approach to identifying "waves" of global development, each of these periods is defined by significant transformations in the scope, scale, and quality of nonviolence's globalization. Lechner's definition of globalization as a process characterized by diffusion, organization, interdependence, and culture and consciousness also helps to frame my historical analysis.

Nonviolence Emerges on the Global Stage

The early wave of the global emergence of this repertoire was marked by three distinct dimensions, which helped to establish its general form and initiate its spread. The first is the conceptualization of the repertoire as global in scope. Early practitioners, visionaries, and cultural entrepreneurs helped to envision and define nonviolence as a form of claims-making that could be universal in application across various countries and social movements. A second important factor was the popular acclaim accorded to movements that helped spread these ideas and techniques to other movements. Cultural entrepreneurs were helpful in this respect, too, as many of them worked as brokers between transnational activists. The publicization of popular movements in international press and media also made indirect emulation of these ideas and techniques more accessible. A third crucial force of this early era was the development of a field of research that helped to establish the repertoire as unique and generalizable. These writers laid the intellectual foundation upon which a more formalized system of strategic action would follow. Upon this foundation, the nonviolence repertoire became increasingly globalized through eras of late and post-Cold War institutionalization as the world experienced a spike in organizations and movements committed to practicing nonviolence.

Early Conceptualization

Peace scholars dig deep into the historical record, presenting plebian strikes against Roman taxation and Confucian teachings as early examples of a primordial method of peaceful resistance (see Lakey 1968; Zunes, Kurtz, and Asher 1999). Indeed, there have been many historical acts of resistance that were not violent, including those Tilly observed in the eighteenth and nineteenth centuries. But the contemporary story almost always begins with Mohandas Mahatma Gandhi, oft considered the "father of nonviolence," because he so extensively theorized and helped to globalize the repertoire of nonviolence practiced today. Indeed, Gandhi was an important cultural entrepreneur (à la Wagner-Pacifici and Schwartz 1991) who presented ideas about claims-making in a new way on the global stage (Ganguly and Docker 2008).

An Indian national, Gandhi was also a cosmopolitan world citizen trained as an attorney at University College, London, where he became part of an English society of vegetarians who drew on Indian culture to formulate their social movement philosophy. After experiencing the racism of South African apartheid first-hand, he delved diligently into the study of active resistance movements around the world. He found inspiration in American abolitionists like Aidan Ballou, who wrote about a biblical form of "nonresistance" that could claim a moral high ground in opposition to injustice. He admired Henry David Thoreau's "Civil Disobedience," an essay on the role of noncooperation in protesting taxes that would be used to fund a war against Mexico. He was moved by Leo Tolstoy's concept of "passive resistance" and founded a "Tolstoy Farm" intentional community in South Africa where residents dedicated themselves to a morally focused life of advocacy for social justice. He borrowed resistance techniques from British suffragists, declaring in 1906 that "they are bound to succeed and gain the franchise, for the simple reason that deeds are better than words" (as cited in Offen, n.d). Although Gandhi would later come to be recognized as an innovator of large nonviolent campaigns, these were based on previous campaigns he had read about in other publications. He studied French resistance against a salt tax, an early Indian cotton boycott, and the organizing efforts of Badshah Khan, a Muslim Pashtun, who first devised a "nonviolent army" in the Northwest Frontier Province of India that later joined Gandhi's civil disobedience movement against the British (Easwaran 1999).[7]

One of the earliest archived international news stories of Gandhi's leading role in the Indian independence movement lays out the principles of Gandhian

---

[7] There were other major movements and movers that engaged with nonviolent tactics (tactics that simply did not require or result in acts of violence) before and around the time of Gandhi's activism. The global labor movement had already enjoyed a brief stint of international organizing that ended in 1914. The union model of organizing through striking, picketing, and rallies had diffused long before international organizational efforts began to emerge. Historical compendiums of nonviolence note the Russian Revolution of 1905 as the first large-scale nonviolent struggle of the twentieth century (see Sharp 2005). Still, Gandhi's entry into the global political arena marks an important shift in how claims-making was organized and how nonviolence came to be conceptualized as a global repertoire.

nonviolence as formulated in his 1919 *satyagraha* campaign to tap into Indian cultural and spiritual practices: "Satyagraha is like a banian tree [sic] with innumerable branches. Civil disobedience is one such branch. Satya (truth) and Ahimsa (non-violence) together make the parent trunk from which all the innumerable branches shoot out" (*The Times of India* 1919). Soon, international support for the Indian independence movement helped to amplify Gandhi's conceptualization of nonviolence globally. The Quakers, who had been present in India since the seventeenth century and opened formal centers there in the late nineteenth century, were quick to establish a Friends of India center in London from which they advocated for the practice of nonviolence in Indian independence and other conflicts. There were many "cosmopolitan translators" who were instrumental in bringing Gandhian thinking on nonviolent resistance to the West. Among them were well-known authors, pastors, politicians, political activists, philanthropists, and educators from Europe and the United States (Scalmer 2011). There was also an expansive movement of early anti-war pacifists who were deeply involved in international peace efforts. This provided a receptive movement structure within which the concept of nonviolence resonated with already established ideals of pacifism while adding new cultural currency to how activists thought about and organized their methods.

At the same time, there was widespread skepticism and debate about the practical limits of such a universalist idea of nonviolence in this early era, illuminating the fits-and-starts of its early conceptualization. Within India, pundits doubted the potential for discipline among the masses and inveighed against the effects of general strikes on Indian workers and regional politicians. When the threat of international war loomed large, global outsiders were dubious that nonviolence could realistically be employed on a global level to deter armed conflict. In World War II, commentators opined that Indian civil disobedience campaigns menaced Allied positions and detracted from the common Indian nationalist and British goal of warding off the threat of Axis imperialism. They challenged the potential for Gandhian nonviolence to combat the violence of Adolf Hitler (to which Gandhi responded by attempting to persuade Hitler to end the war in person) or even to quell the smaller scale violence that characterized ethnic conflicts within India. Nevertheless, support for the nonviolence repertoire continued to spread among a core network of international activists. As early as 1921, news archives record public proclamations of a commitment to nonviolence "like that of Mr. Gandhi" by the Burmese independence movement, whose leaders claimed that "Ours is a noble fight, a fight against domination and other rule. Our doctrine is 'right is might' not 'might is right' " (*Los Angeles Times* 1921). Soon after, leaders of the Egyptian independence movement also committed themselves to nonviolence and the targets of their nonviolent resistance began to fear imminent changes in their status:

> Word has reached London that Nationalist leaders are thinking of introducing the nonviolent, noncooperationist methods of the Gandhians of India – methods already such a blight on certain British industries – into the villages along the banks of the Nile. Is it not the threat of nonviolence that makes Britain reiterate so sharply her desire to make Egypt free? (*Boston Daily Globe* 1922)

The concept of nonviolence easily diffused into contexts with favorable cultural logics (Strang and Soule 1998). An international community that had long contemplated other forms of passive resistance against the threat of international war quickly vowed allegiance to "nonviolence" and "active resistance."[8] A. J. Muste was one exemplary early peace leader with the international Fellowship of Reconciliation who was involved with labor organizing in the United States as well as advocating for pacifism in the face of World War I. Muste would enthusiastically embrace Gandhi's teachings that nonviolence must be understood as both the means and the ends of peace and justice movements, famously stating that "There is no way to peace. Peace is the way" (Danielson 2014). As early as the 1922 International Women's League for Peace and Freedom meeting, presider Jane Addams called on activists to use "nonviolence" as a means for ending war. She was among many conscientious objectors to adopt this terminology. The US peace, labor, and early civil rights movements also began considering Gandhi's philosophy and principles of nonviolence as a model they could emulate in their advocacy work (Chabot 2000; Diwakar and Nidhi 1964).

Prominent Indian activists made several international trips to promote the nonviolence philosophy as a generally beneficial method of action, both on their own initiative and by invitation (Scalmer 2011). In the early 1920s, for example, Indian independence activist and noted literary figure Rabindranath Tagore was invited to China amid a series of silk-worker strikes to give a lecture on the importance of nonviolence (Beck 2008). Christian ministers spoke of Gandhi as

---

[8] The long history of global peace organizing should also be noted as an important precursor. Following the Treaty of Vienna in 1814, peace societies sprang up all over Europe and some parts of Asia in the mid-1800s. The first series of world peace conferences were held between 1843 and 1853 (Boulding 2000). Organizations developed in the 1860s to work toward an international peace movement became very active in the 1870s and 1880s (Beales 1931). Since the 1860s, the Quakers have also had long-established "Friends" communities that have worked for peace in India, Madagascar, West China, Ceylon, and Syria (Friends Service Council 1947). These early networks would later become active conduits for the international diffusion of nonviolence (Scalmer 2011).

"The Christ of Today" for his methods of personal suffering in commitment to the truth (Walker 1967).

In 1939, Maude Royden, a former suffragist and English pastor, worked with other peace activists to draft and submit a formal proposal to the League of Nations for a nonviolent "Peace Army" to intercede following the Japanese invasion of the Chinese province of Manchuria. Although the proposal gained global attention through its worldwide publication in newspapers in the United States to Sierra Leone, allowing the organization to recruit nearly one thousand volunteers, it failed to receive a UN institutional mandate. Several years later, the League of Nations was able to place only a few volunteers in the Palestinian territories. Still, Royden's vision sparked a steady stream of continuing efforts to consider how best to export nonviolent intervention (Moser-Puangsuwan and Weber 2000).

More formal efforts to globalize nonviolence emerged through the writing of scholars and philosophers, many of which remain canonical statements on the repertoire's universal applicability. Sociologist Clarence Case completed his doctoral thesis on Gandhi in 1919 and later published an extensive historical analysis of the Christian roots and social-psychological dynamics of nonviolent action (Case 1923). Numerous books contemplating the universal appeal of Ghandi's formulation of a nonviolent resistance followed soon after. Exemplary among these is *Ghandi*, published in 1924 by Nobel Prize recipient Romain Rolland, known at the time as "the conscience of Europe." This book, translated into over twenty languages, was considered an authoritative treatment of the workings of the *Mahatma*, or great soul, and was one of the first biographies framed for a Western audience. In it, Rolland expounds upon how Gandhi's cultural background and social experiences shaped world politics.

Also notable among early efforts to globalize nonviolence were Gregg's (1935) *The Power of Non-violence*, which outlines a general theory of conditions under which nonviolence is effective, and Krishnalal Shridharani's 1939 *War without Violence*, which delineates the logics of satyagraha. Gregg's discussion begins by using the Gandhian movement as an initial example before delving into a deeper discussion of the role of morality in nonviolent conflict and conflict resolution. He insists that this process of nonviolence is ultimately universal:

> With it, every single individual of every race, nation, occupation, and all ages above infancy, can do something real and immediate and continuous for the cause of peace, without waiting for any other person or organisation to do something first. It suddenly becomes clear that the work of saving humanity does not rest with the great leaders but begins and continues with one of us. (Gregg 1935, 189)

Gregg's book ends with a proposal for the development of self-discipline through group training programs that would make peace accessible to all people. In this sense, the book also presented a bridge between early conceptualization and later systematization efforts. Unsurprisingly, it was a highly consulted text for second wave nonviolence theorists.

Shridharani's framework of Gandhian nonviolence as a general system of resistance also set a new kind of precedent for thinking systematically about the strategic potential of nonviolence. He mapped out the social and political conditions and techniques that brought about a successful nonviolent direct-action campaign for social change and identified a set of progressive stages through which nonviolence leads to social change.

Both texts would soon become programmatic for a new generation of nonviolence globalizers, although discourse about nonviolence did not reach universal agreement. There were many ongoing disputes about its applicability in certain kinds of conflicts – the horrors of World War II would long linger on the contemplative minds of nonviolence theorists. However, nonviolence continued to globalize in a more systematic and formally organized fashion. The international network that had come to support nonviolence efforts in India and abroad began to shift gears from asking how nonviolence could be generally conceptualized to figuring out how to formally implement nonviolence in a growing number of movements and organizations. Thus, this early era was pivotal in formulating the understanding of how and why the repertoire could be considered best claims-making practice through the concerted efforts of repertoire developers. But new and expanded efforts would be needed to grow nonviolence's practice beyond the noble experiments of the era in which it originated.

Post-World War II Systematization and the Rise of Nonviolence Emissaries

Several significant events spurred the nonviolence repertoire's move from its early conceptualization into its postwar period of systematization. First, many of the major independence movements that the global nonviolence movement had rallied around ended around this time. New independence movements and movements focused on other causes necessitated new ways of implementing nonviolence. This entailed deriving general lessons from the Indian and other early era models to map nonviolence onto new contexts. Second, these movements became increasingly international through more formal means of organization. The global organizational dimension of nonviolence blossomed in the postwar era through the proliferation of new organizations explicitly dedicated to spreading nonviolent protest tactics and notable individuals who dedicated their lives to building up these networks, working as international emissaries of a global movement for nonviolence. Third, while nonviolence continued to be a principal organizing framework for the world peace movement, there was a substantive shift in the concerns of international peace activists. At this time, attention moved from nonviolent resistance to the world wars toward disarmament during the Cold War arms race, necessitating the development of new forms of direct-action protest and demonstrations. And fourth, there was a noticeable change in the tenor of nonviolence discourse. While some authors continued to write about Gandhi, many more directed their attention to forging a new field of nonviolent studies focused on the general repertoire of nonviolence and its extension into new political arenas. Part of this movement splintered off into a secularized and clinical concept of nonviolence, still salient today in frequently published research on civil resistance studies. Also at this time, activists developed tactical manuals for nonviolence as a universally applicable repertoire that could be systematically outlined, organized, implemented, and evaluated. The field of nonviolence became so systematized in this postwar era that many smaller nonviolence movements emerged as well, crystalizing a global movement of movements using nonviolent tactics.

Following World War II, international efforts to systematize nonviolence unfolded through several notable global historical transformations. During the war years of the 1940s, there had been broad societal efforts to resist fascism. Notable nonviolent resistance efforts unfolded in Norway, Denmark, France, and Berlin (Sharp 2005). These occurred through an amalgamation of social forces, the enactment of tactics at hand or already being employed by other civilians, the principles of faith, and knowledge of Gandhi's approach (Paxton 2011). Gandhi had in fact publicly weighed in on how nonviolence could be mobilized against Hitler (Kling 1991). Major general strikes also occurred in Ecuador, Honduras, and Nicaragua, and brought down dictatorships in El Salvador and Guatemala in 1944.

Interestingly, the United States played a role in widespread "informational campaigns" throughout Central American during this era, where the Atlantic Charter signaled a shift away from direct military interventions in the region toward the promotion of democratic governments in which people should be guaranteed the right to redress (van den Berk 2018). The so-called "Four Freedoms" of the charter served as an inspiration for anti-colonial movements around the world, though not without other forms of political diplomatic influence by powerful nations seeking to support the election of favorable leaders, as van den Berk (2018) also explains. This iterative development of political and civic form is something Tilly (1993) described in his study of contentious repertoires in

Great Britain. Social movements, he explains, "parallel and feed on electoral politics, precisely because they signal the presence of mass support," which democratically elected leaders must learn to cultivate to maintain power. A global view allows us to see the messy fits and starts of a nonviolent orientation in which changes in the structure of the polity sometimes institutionalized nonviolent politics as an expected and permissible expression of citizenship and, in other cases, nonviolent movements demanded the kinds of democratic governance that would correspond with the nonviolent redress of grievances.

In 1957, the same year Dr. Martin Luther King Jr. established the Southern Christian Leadership Conference, anti-colonial movements in Africa found new strategic power in nonviolence, which escalated into a major general strike in South Africa and in Ghana. Revolutionary leader Kwame Nkrumah (who would become president, post-independence) claimed inspiration from Gandhian satyagraha as he helped to mobilize an independence movement motivated by the concept of "positive action." In this way, he aimed to counter the deficit model of colonial transitions with a Gandhian emphasis on positive social reconstruction. Nkrumah began working to export a general African nonviolent model for independence, proclaiming that "without African independence, the freedom of Ghana is meaningless," epitomizing what Robertson (1992) called the "particularization of the universal," an intentional process of taking a global form and making it unique to a local context. Nkrumah helped to organize a series of African independence conferences in Ghana intended to build strategic and tactical networks between Pan-African nonviolence leaders. These were attended by over three hundred delegates from more than sixty-five organizations (Sutherland and Meyer 2000). Soon, kindred African independence leaders began organizing movements based on a public commitment to nonviolence. Kenneth Kaunda of Zambia and Jomo Kenyatta of Kenya were among the most visible of these leaders.

In the United States, civil rights activists had long been interested in the methods and philosophy of Gandhi. Indian exiles, traveling speakers, and international peace journals publicized new developments in Gandhi's tactical nonviolence. In the 1930s, African American leaders, among them Howard Thurman and Benjamin Mays of Howard University, traveled to India to see Gandhian nonviolence in action and open a dialogue about the potential for a mass nonviolent movement for civil rights in the US South (see also Sheehan 2021). Gandhi was so invested in the success of this effort that he began to view the civil rights movement as the next major portal through which nonviolence would be globalized, commenting that "It may be through the Negroes that the unadulterated message of nonviolence will be delivered to our world" (Sibley 1967). While the earliest noncooperation actions in the United States were launched at the same time as Gandhi's globally acclaimed Salt March in 1930, it took another decade to mobilize widespread nonviolent resistance in the United States. When that did finally happen, the US civil rights movement became a major political event of international importance (Spence 2011), and its leaders joined Gandhi as canonical forefathers of the new global repertoire (Gaines 2007). In 1960 alone, over 300 sit-in desegregation strikes were recorded around the United States (Andrews and Biggs 2006).

Unique to this new era was the systematic way in which civil rights activists prepared for nonviolent action, which in turn advanced its global diffusion. Beginning in the mid-1940s, post-World War II activists modeled and adapted Gandhian techniques for nonviolence training in what sociologist and civil rights scholar Morris (1984) referred to as movement "halfway houses," crucial networking and mobilization sites where activists transmitted tactical knowledge and skills (see Chabot 2000).[9] Direct US-Indian ties, the US emulation of Indian tactics, and civil rights leaders' discursive commitment to nonviolence cemented the "reinvention of the Gandhian repertoire" in an African American context. This allowed for the formulation of a generalizable recipe for social change in the United States founded upon strong moral principles (Chabot 2011).

Another surge in nonviolent movements marked the next several decades moving into the late 1960s, including uprising by student, workers', independence, democracy, and human rights movements. In Latin America, democratic initiatives moved across Honduras, Bolivia, and Brazil, where activists expressed a commitment to *firmenza permanente* or "relentless persistence" (McManus and Schlabach 1991). Later, nonviolent movements resisted brutal military repression in Argentina and Chile. In Africa, conflicts over independence resulted in violent civil wars, but nonviolence remained a part of many resistance efforts, especially in Mali and Senegal (Darboe 2010; Nesbitt and Zunes 2009). In Asia, the same violent-nonviolent tension persisted, with groups in West Papua and East Timor holding fast to nonviolence, as did student movements in Japan and Korea (Choi 1999; MacLeod 2015; Mason 2005; Salla 1995; Tsurami 1970). The late 1960s saw a burgeoning civil society movement in Palestine and major nonviolent resistance movements in Greece, Portugal, and the Basque country.

---

[9] One of the first highly visible civil rights protests was the 1947 Freedom Ride, which entailed an extensive two-day training that presented activists with a number of protest scenarios. The participants were asked to contemplate, "What if the bus driver insulted you? What if you were actually assaulted? What if the police threatened you?" The trainers and trainees proceeded to simulate and work through these and other scenarios by taking on the roles of the bus drivers, "hysterical segregationists," police, and protesting participants (Hare and Blumberg 1968, 51). As mobilization for the movement ramped up, this kind of training became more widespread, systematically preparing activists for boycotts, sit-ins, marches, demonstrations, and a range of other protest and noncooperation techniques.

In the United States, the nonviolence repertoire transformed the organization of farmworkers in the West under the leadership of Cesar Chavez and Dolores Huerta, who wove Gandhian ethics into a Mexican revolutionary narrative about the rights of immigrant laborers. Resistance against the Vietnam War and the second wave of women's rights activism were organized under the auspices of nonviolence. Each of these movements drew on the nonviolent repertoire and the increasingly systematic ways in which nonviolent tactics came to be organized within that repertoire (Echols 2019; Long 2021; Swerdlow 1993).

While the world wars lingered on the global consciousness of the peace movement, activists witnessed the construction of a new type of conflict in the build up to the Cold War. Fearing the next major global battle would have even more disastrous effects, a great deal of international attention among nonviolence theorists and practitioners immediately turned toward the issue of disarmament. The proliferation of arms and nuclear weapons during the Cold War compelled activists to think more deeply about the moral framework for global nonviolence (Meyer 1990; Wittner 2009), sparking an "intensification of consciousness of the world as a whole" (Robertson 1992, 8). When Hungarian physicist Leo Szilard drafted and disseminated his now famous petition against the United States's use of the atomic bomb among some of the world's leading scientists, including his mentor Albert Einstein, he shaped collective fears about an "era of devastation on an unimaginable scale" (Szilard 1945).

In the 1950s, a series of disarmament conferences were organized in which activists envisioned a new global nonviolence movement. The goals of this movement were twofold: to raise global awareness of the buildup of arms and to develop direct action tactics to halt the arms race (Sibley 1963). In the United States, the Committee for Nonviolent Action (CNVA) became a central network through which major actions were developed. The orientation of "most of the leadership" was "strongly imbued with Gandhian ideas" about the best strategy for claims-making (Sibley 1963). Actions were sometimes locally implemented, but often transnational in organization and scope. In other instances, borders were physically crossed during nonviolent actions to target the locations associated with the buildup, stockpiling, or testing of weaponry. The CNVA was especially productive in innovating highly visible and daring techniques, such as sending ships into nuclear test zones in the late 1950s and early 1960s, holding vigils at factories where arms were produced, staging a global walk against proliferation from San Francisco to Moscow in 1960, a walk from Québec to Washington to Guantánamo in 1963, and leading a series of "imaginative and dramatic protest demonstrations" to call attention to the alarming rate of arms production during the Cold War (Sibley 1963).

This action intensive movement helped to expand strategic efforts toward systematization as it began to develop a nonviolent alternative to nuclear proliferation. The core groups of peace activists involved in this network carried specific tactical schemas into new political organizing fields and generated an expanding cache of tactical manuals and workshop training models (Sibley 1963). Antiproliferation of nuclear power movements that drew heavily on a nonviolence framework developed in the UK and Germany over the 1980s. These movements galvanized new thinking about the possibility for the extinction – or large-scale obliteration – of the human race in the face of nuclear war. This consciousness folded into a newly emerging environmental movement (Schell 2000) that has also come to employ nonviolence as its strategic and tactical guiding framework (Downey 1986).

International organizations also contributed significantly to the systematization and diffusion of the nonviolence repertoire during this second wave, leading to the building up of an extensive network of nonviolence specialists. In the postwar period, there was a rapid growth of INGOs explicitly dedicated to spreading and supporting nonviolence. By the late 1940s, Gandhi and other nonviolence activists were working to establish a peace brigade to address the threat of violence amidst ethnic antagonists in India. Gandhi was assassinated by one such ethnic extremist just two weeks before the brigade's inaugural meeting. The idea finally came to fruition when Vinoba Bhave organized the *Shanti Sena* army in 1957 (Shepard 1987). Then, meetings of international peacemakers in Delhi (the War Resisters International triennial, where plans for a new organization were drafted) and later in Beirut led to the development of the World Peace Brigade (WPB) with the goal of implementing nonviolence interventions across national borders. This was conceived as a "natural outgrowth of internationalizing the forces of nonviolence" (Walker in PBI Archives).[10] Activists focused on four aspects deemed priorities for constructing such a global organization: encouraging the practice of Gandhian nonviolence, transnationalizing support for the peace movement in US and Europe, nonviolent social justice struggles (including the US civil rights movement), and movements for national independence and reconstruction (PBI Archives). World Peace Brigade helped to facilitate nonviolence efforts in Indian, Chinese, Turkish, and Cyprian conflicts as well as in Zambia (then Rhodesia) before dissolving and reorganizing as PBI. From 1961 to 1981, the WPB was involved in a number of internationally organized events. WPB activists spent several years supporting the mobilization of the Pan-African independence movement.

---

[10] World Peace Brigade organizers credit the idea of a peace brigade to Gandhi's 1906 suggestion for a "nonviolent army" (PBI Archives), which he later revived in his vision for an Indian nonviolent force that could help in national defense during the world wars (Shephard 1987).

They set up a nonviolent tactics training center in Dar es Salaam on the front lines of the Zambian freedom movement and worked to build transnational support for several important marches and protest efforts there. They also planned a march on Northern Rhodesia and organized the Delhi to Peking Friendship Walk after conflict broke out on the India–China border. The organization dissolved a few years after its founding, but activists connected to WPB helped to negotiate and maintain a ceasefire during the 1962–1974 Nagaland conflict in Northern India. In 1971, organizers went to help in the crisis area that eventually became Bangladesh. From 1972 to 1974, former WPB activists were among an international group that launched an extensive Cyprus Resettlement Project to help resettle five thousand Greek and twenty thousand Turkish refugees fleeing violence in 1963.

At that time, there had been steady involvement from international activists in a number of actions, including the Sahara Project protest against French nuclear testing in the Sahara desert, the San Francisco to Moscow Walk for Peace against nuclear proliferation, and the string of independence efforts beginning to develop in East and Central Africa.

Pre-existing peace organizations that participated in the early conceptualization of nonviolence like War Resisters International (WRI) and the International Fellowship for Reconciliation (IFOR) also placed nonviolence specialists in new conflict zones and helped to spread a general model for teaching and implementing nonviolence. This was an important process for seeding new regional organizations that facilitated local mobilization on one level and strengthened transnational ties to global civil society on another. The work of two active IFOR activists, Hildegard Goss-Mayr and her husband Jean Goss, in Latin America, for example, resulted in the establishment of the Servicio Paz y Justicia para America Latina (the Latin American Peace and Justice Service, or SERPAJ) in 1974. SERPAJ is a regionally focused but transnationally networked organization that was extensively involved in mobilizing resistance movements in Argentina, Brazil, Bolivia, and Uruguay. Several IFOR and WRI members also worked extensively in Africa, providing tactical consulting for the Upper Volta River project and helping to organize independence efforts in Tanganyika and Zambia.

International organizational efforts to place volunteers in conflicts zones throughout the world helped to formally spread common knowledge and skills related to nonviolence. As interested outsiders investing in the repertoire's diffusion, international volunteers also helped to legitimate the use of nonviolence as a desirable and effective means of claims-making. Additional examples from the 1950s, 1960s, and 1970s include peaceworker volunteers sent to Africa, Asia, and North and South America; Peace Service Units throughout Europe; IFOR's Project Eirene in North and Central America, Europe, and Africa; the Sahara

Protest Team in Algeria; World Peace Brigade efforts in Zambia, Rhodesia, and Tanzania; the San Francisco to Moscow Walk for Peace; the Delhi to Peking Friendship March; the Québec-Washington-Guantánamo Walk for Peace; the Nagaland Peace Mission in East India; and the Cyprus Resettlement Project (Moser-Puangsuwan and Weber 2000). International conferences helped to raise awareness of the global prospects for nonviolence. In his history of the founding of PBI, Walker points to earlier conferences in 1961 in India and in 1962 in Addis Ababa, as well as three important conferences in Costa Rica in 1971, Driebergen in 1972, and India on the twenty-fifth anniversary of Gandhi's death in 1973. In 1977, there was an International Seminar on Training for Nonviolent Action in Mexico. Each of these efforts constituted pivotal moments in the development of the global nonviolence movement into a supra-regional network of peacemakers.

During this second wave of development, supporters of nonviolent studies wove together insights from activists directly involved in major movements and organizations with the principles of social science to create a dynamic field of study on how nonviolent protest affects power and social change. Several scholars from the early era of nonviolence's conceptualization further contributed to the systematization of analytical thinking on nonviolence in the second era. Richard Gregg's *Power of Nonviolence* was reprinted in 1959 with a new forward by Martin Luther King Jr., who had also just published his own reflections on the topic in *Stride toward Freedom* (1958). Clarence Case and several of his students (among them Paul Hare and Charles Chatfield) helped to establish a new focus on the social psychological dimensions of waging nonviolent conflict (Blumberg, Hare, and Coston 2006; Chatfield 1973).

In 1950, the German ethnologist W. E. Muhlmann published *Mahatma Gandhi: Der Mann, sein Werk, und seine Wirkung*, a book which was influential in shaping how European scholars began to understand both the nature of conflict and the possibilities for engineering conflict resolution nonviolently. In Norway, as the Norwegian government launched a technical assistance project in southern India, the scholar Arne Næss began what would become a formative study of Gandhian nonviolence and conflict resolution techniques. In collaboration with now renowned peace studies scholar Johan Galtung, Næss undertook a series of writing projects that culminated in the publication of the Norwegian-language *Gandhis politiske etikk* in 1955, published in English as *Gandhi in the Nuclear Age* in 1965, and *Gandhi and Group Conflict* in 1974 (Galtung 2011a).

In the United States in 1957, Jessie Bernard developed a sociological argument against assumptions that individuals were either intrinsically prone to violence or nonviolence based on the assertion that nonviolence was something that could be socially engineered. That same year, *The Journal of Conflict Resolution* was established, providing an academic venue for discussing these ideas. In 1959, the

Peace Research Institute was established in Oslo. In 1964, the Peace Research Association was founded and established *The Journal of Peace Research*, a journal that continues to feature prominent studies of nonviolent movements today.

Scholars were also prolifically publishing books that compiled numerous case studies of nonviolent movements, explored the various mechanisms that worked across contexts, and expounded upon the philosophical implications of nonviolence for creating a good society. In 1963, *The Quiet Battle* by Mulford Sibley considered whether these assertions of classic texts were reflected in nonviolent movements in the United States and South Africa, disarmament, and the potential for a nonviolent national defense force. In 1967, *Gandhi: His Relevance for Our Times* examined the factors that instantiated the successes and failures of the Indian independence movement and contemplated "the ideal and the actual" in Gandhi's philosophy, as well as the application of nonviolence in the US civil rights, disarmament, and antiwar movements (Ramachandran and Mahadevan 1967). In 1968, American sociologists Paul Hare and Herbert Blumberg (1968) organized a now canonical collection of sociological analyses of various critical cases and the general sociological process of change galvanized by nonviolent techniques.

Among these influential authors were Joan Bondurant, who has published prolifically on Gandhian methods and tactics; George Lakey, whose sociological treatise on the "mechanisms of nonviolent action" pioneered the translation of sociological analysis into practical and systematically devised plans of action; and Gene Sharp, now affectionately known as the "godfather of nonviolence." Lakey's published works are highly esteemed archival evidence of this era of systematization. Through his direct involvement in the US civil rights movement to his more recent work on environmental justice campaigns, Lakey has given more than six hundred consultations and training seminars in more than thirty countries. He developed a talent for translating social theories into action guides early on, publishing the seminal manual for nonviolent resistance, *Strategy for a Living Revolution,* in 1973. This guide provided insight from the reflective action ethos of a Movement for a New Society (MNS). The MNS was a nonviolent revolutionary movement in the United States that brought together activists for various causes in the late 1970s to contemplate how nonviolence could be used to construct a new society, much like Gandhi did with his *satyagraha ashrams* (Cornell 2011). Today, Lakey is still a phenomenally prolific nonviolent journalist, writer, speaker, activist, and trainer.

Gene Sharp's work also contributed tremendously to the development of the field, formalizing a systematic and political science-based approach to studying nonviolent strategic efficacy. His catalog of tactics has been distributed worldwide, earning him the insurrectionist's honor of being banned by numerous autocratic regimes (Engler 2013). Sharp was an anti-conscription activist during the Korean War and was involved in various nonviolent peace movements in the late 1950s. In 1960, he published a book expressing his sentiments on nonviolence, *Gandhi Wields the Moral Weapon of Power*. He later earned his doctorate in political theory at Oxford in 1968, funded by a special US Department of Defense program. In 1973, he elaborated on his dissertation research in *The Politics of Nonviolent Action*, a three-volume opus on power and struggle and the dynamics and methods of nonviolent action. In this highly lauded book, Sharp's major contributions were generally delineating multiple sources of power in any one society and providing a typology for the ways in which nonviolent action can successfully redirect that power in the favor of claims-makers. Sharp continued to write prolifically, becoming a canonical figure in the field of nonviolent studies.

Nonviolent studies continued to grow as an interdisciplinary field, fostering a dynamic exchange among academics and practitioners. Leaders of major nonviolent movements came together to identify the generalist strands of their methods for a global movement through the 1977 publication of *The Struggle for Humanity: Agents of Nonviolent Change in a Violent World* (Hope and Young 1977). Academic work continued in this era with Hare and Blumberg's *Liberation without Violence* (1977), which categorically examined third-party nonviolent interventions, and Bruyn and Rayman's *Nonviolent Action and Social Change* (1979), which presented a theory of nonviolence as a system of generalizable protest tactics and first-hand accounts from organizers from a global array of movements.

Feminist nonviolent activists of this era debated the intersection of women's liberation and nonviolence, adding a uniquely feminist framework to thinking about nonviolence's potential for transforming systems of oppression, patriarchy, and war (McAllister 1982). Magazines and journals of prominent nonviolent organizations like War Resisters League's *WIN Magazine* hosted special issues about topics such as "Feminism and Pacifism" and "Nonviolent Rape Resistance." The London Women's Liberation Workshop published a special issue exploring feminism and nonviolence, the US social justice network MNS hosted a gathering on feminism and nonviolence and later many of these women joined the Feminism and Nonviolence Working Group and attended an international gathering on women and nonviolence hosted by the International Fellowship of Reconciliation in France. Feminists also contributed to the growing women's self-defense movement of the 1970s by offering nonviolent defense strategies, classes, manuals, and other techniques (Gallo-Cruz, forthcoming).

The efforts of these and many other activists wholly dedicated to the spread of nonviolence helped to systematize this now global repertoire. Here, my research details an aspect of repertoire emergence Tilly's has not: the discursive articulation of the repertoire. This extensive cultural theorization imbues the repertoire with meaning about why and how this particular repertoire is best practice for democratic claims-making, emblematic of the consciousness expanding work of world culture (Lechner and Boli 2005). As the globalization of nonviolence progressed in the decades to come, this consciousness raising work would continue in new, more specialized ways. With systematization in theory and practice came more formal modes of organization and ultimately the professionalization of a global nonviolence civil society network.

Early and High Institutionalization

The ways in which nonviolence has become institutionalized is significant not only to a fuller historical understanding of the global dynamics of repertoire emergence, but also to analysis of how and why nonviolence works in different contexts and time periods. Established models of behavior constrain opportunities for action and make them more predictable, even across unique political contexts (Prujit and Roggeband 2014; Rucht and Neidhardt 2002). Thus, institutionalization can cause "path dependence" within resistance movements as they increasingly follow culturally available and legitimate – or, "scripted" – recipes for action. This process also tends to cement the esteem, influence, and authority of particular roles and actors (Giugni and Grasso 2015; Staggenborg 2013). Predictability matters to movements because it removes much of what was formerly unexpected and unplanned for in contentious interactions (Meyer and Tarrow 1998), a force of power nonviolent theorists have long identified as central to the effectiveness of this repertoire. This allows the targets of resistance to prepare counter-movement or demobilization strategies. Therefore, as nonviolence becomes more institutionalized at the global level, widespread knowledge of the repertoire's practices reduces the potential for nonviolent "jiu-jitsu" maneuvers Gregg (1935) identified that capitalize on the element of the unexpected.

The turn from systematization to institutionalization can be identified by two sociological features: the development of rule-like patterns of prescribed approaches to mobilization and the embedding of these approaches into formal authoritative structures, such as professional organizations (Zucker 1987, 444). The prior era of systematization laid a favorable foundation for nonviolence's institutionalization in both respects. The extensive work done to formally develop a replicable nonviolent approach to political action, the creation of formalized training programs, the nonviolence initiatives led by global and professional organizations, and the development of an academic field of study funded by high-profile organizations all helped to define the repertoire. This established a cache of documented and tested techniques that could then be generally applied and supported by a growing network of professionalized authorities.

Movements had much to gain from practicing nonviolence during this era of institutionalization. In Latin America, for example, the establishment of SERPAJ in 1974 and the work of its president, Argentinian 1980 Nobel Peace Prize recipient Adolfo Perez Esquivel, brought international attention to the nonviolent demonstrations of the Madres de Plaza de Mayo, who protested against torture and disappearances in Argentina. The Catholic Church's election of a Polish pope in 1978 and his public support for the nonviolent actions of the Polish Solidarity movement in 1980 also led to a Nobel Peace Prize for organizer Lech Walesa. This helped boost morale for the movement, which would celebrate the end of the Soviet occupation of Poland in 1989. The South African movement against discrimination and, eventually, apartheid experienced several waves of nonviolent action across decades of mobilization efforts, all of which proved successful with the fall of apartheid in 1994. Furthermore, national movements that emerged in the 1980s through the 1990s and 2000s helped to usher in a new, global wave of democracy (Markoff 1996). This shift in global politics saw the end of dictatorships in Latin America and the fall of the Eastern Bloc in Europe.

The foundings of new international nonviolent organizations had already begun to grow in the post-war period, joining established peace organizations in working to spread the repertoire on a global scale. However, this number of foundings expanded again in the 1980s into the 2000s, as illustrated in Figure 1.

Qualitative analysis of their programmatic objectives and activities reveals that these organizations became a professionalized means of diffusing the repertoire

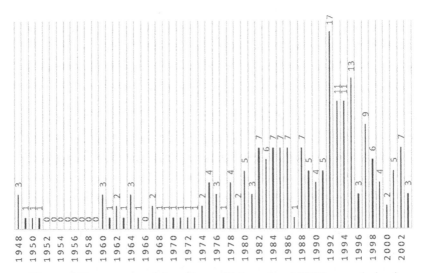

Figure 1 Data on annual foundings of international NGOs was derived from the Union of International Associations Yearbook

and they also became more varied in their objectives during this period. Through the 1970s, nonviolence organizations generally focused on the promotion of nonviolence and the development of training programs. In the 1980s, there was a rapid expansion into specific campaigns and conflicts. Their global reach also grew, as indicated by the increase in these organizations' memberships over time. Figures 2 and 3 depict a shift from a membership base that is predominantly located in the Global North to one increasingly involving the Global South.[11]

The increase in nonviolence INGO membership in the Global South speaks to these organizations' distinct orientation toward building up the resources and capacities of struggling democracies and civil societies.[12] Nonviolence INGOs may also engage in the kind of direct diplomacy and intergovernmental advocacy work targeted by many other INGOs, but these are often secondary objectives.

Qualitative reports on nonviolent organizations help to illustrate how INGOs diffuse a global strategic action repertoire into different local contexts. These INGOs impart repertoire knowledge and skills through sharing training, discourse, and tactics with local activists. Organizations like PBI and Witness for Peace were active in monitoring abuses against civil society in Central America in the 1980s. When providing witness, nonviolent INGOs strategically place first-world citizen observers in conflict zones to deter repression by local authorities considered to be illegitimate on the global stage. PBI began its first formal field project in Guatemala, for example, in 1983. This project was initiated in response to a long period of military repression rooted in dictatorial actions spanning back to the 1970s. Over the decades to follow, PBI supported local civil society in a variety of ways. They provided protective accompaniment to ensure the safety of organizers at risk of disappearance or death; supplied international observers to help hold the Guatemalan government accountable to civil society, intergovernmental agencies, and countries that it wished to maintain amicable political relations with; and offered education, training, and guidance to support the practice of effective nonviolence by local movements. All of this work involved sharing a cultural framework rooted in Gandhian ideals of fairness and right process, a distinct political language of human rights, and the structure of Western representative democracy. On a cultural level, PBI helped to articulate the

---

[11] The connections between nonviolence INGOs and local movements may be openly documented or confidential depending on the political cost of ties to organizations that support resistance in certain contexts. In my fieldwork and interviews with prominent representatives of nonviolence nongovernmental organizations, I learned of several projects that were strategically incognito due to the safety risks faced by organizers.

[12] This trend is not without criticism. Increasingly, critics have raised questions about the cultural content and power dynamics created by global nonviolence organizations seeking to build democracies that favor neoliberal political economies oriented toward Western power. These organizations have also been accused of choosing to train and support movements that favor the empowerment of new regimes of elites (cf. Eschle and Stammers 2004).

Contentious Politics

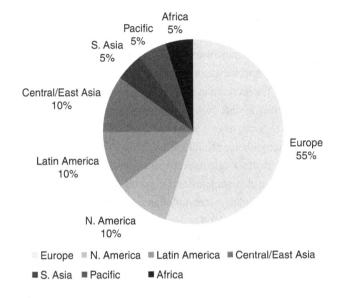

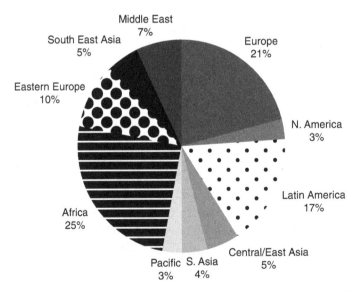

Figure 2 and Figure 3 Data on regional membership in nonviolence INGOs was derived from the Union of International Associations Yearbook

expectations and norms of field engagement, constitute ideals of activist entitle-ments that could inform political demands, and promote best practice for making demands and redressing grievances in line with the increasingly codified practice of nonviolence (Gallo-Cruz 2016b).

This solidarity work diffuses the repertoire by offering local leaders a new way of thinking about and acting on behalf of their own interests, even if it does so by offering new ideas of what kinds of rights and privileges local organizers could demand. This does not necessarily erase local understandings and orientations, a common criticism that nonviolent INGOs actively work to avoid. In the same way that learning a new language allows new frameworks for organizing ideas and new opportunities for social connection, the diffusion of nonviolence helps cultivate a "global grassroots" of interconnected solidarity networks and common ideas about justice and conflict resolution (Gallo-Cruz 2016b).

Nonviolence organizational studies also reveal that the world of formal training grew significantly throughout this period of early and late institutional-ization. Global consultants have held countless training sessions on nonviolent civil resistance tactics with activists around the world. In my fieldwork with Nonviolence International in 2009, I marveled at the wall full of shelves of nonviolent tactical training manuals from decades of action in countries across the globe, recently published in a collection entitled *Civil Resistance Tactics in the 21st Century* (Beer 2021). The editor, Michael Beer, along with Gene Sharp and George Lakey, was an early movement trainer in Burma in the 1980s.

The institutionalization of nonviolence as a global repertoire accelerated from 1989 into the 1990s and 2000s. This acceleration was marked by a surge in high-profile independence movements that helped to bring about the fall of the Eastern Bloc and an end to the first Cold War; significant expansion of a professionalized industry for training and supporting nonviolent movements; deeper study of nonviolence in academia; and the continued celebration of the nonviolence repertoire by the United Nations and international bodies.

In my examination of 117 major movements drawing on established nonvio-lent approaches in the post-World War II era, I found that only twenty-eight emerged and resolved by the end of 1979, thirty-three movements were active through or emerged during the 1980s, and fifty-six movements mobilized in 1989 or later. A new wave of independence motivated many movements in the 1980s. At this time, nonviolent collective action techniques were often seen by independence organizers as the only approach to bringing about democracy. Furthermore, social learning of the nonviolent repertoire occurred in this era through direct and formal initiatives as well as the indirect and informal adoption of what was considered to be best practice in organizing social movements. This occurred both as movements emulated the approaches of other organizations and through direct support provided by transnational solidarity networks, formal training, and advocacy by international organizations.

The International Center for Nonviolent Conflict (ICNC), founded in 2002 by Peter Ackerman, one of Gene Sharp's former students, is exemplary of this post-Cold War era of high institutionalization. ICNC offers training to activists and organizations around the world. It works on major movements and revolutionary initiatives, from the resistance against Slobodan Milošević in former Yugoslavia to diaspora mobilization against the Islamic government in Iran. The International Center for Nonviolent Conflict has gained additional visibility through the rapid professionalization of the nonviolence strategic consultation industry. This work is due in large part to an endowment from Ackerman, a successful "junk bonds" investor who returned to his early academic roots by using his personal wealth to fund an international nonviolent action organization. This large endowment distinguishes ICNC from the other nonviolence INGOs whose organizers I interviewed as a part of this study. Many of the other organizations are supported by ongoing donations including grants and small gifts collected at parties and speaking events and may stretch those dollars through cost-saving measures such as using personal living quarters for professional work. In contrast, ICNC maintains a high-profile executive office near prominent political and economically well-endowed organizations like the International Monetary Fund, the Kennedy Center, and the Saudi Arabian Embassy.

The International Center for Nonviolent Conflict also holds a high place in the development of the global nonviolence repertoire as they have published prolifically in the field and sponsor many academic endeavors, though these sponsorships require allowing ICNC employees to direct events and take editorial control over publications and data. They have solicited many academic stars to praise the success of nonviolent action in democratic movements at public events and to create reports and design trainings for their programs. The International Center for Nonviolent Conflict has become well-networked among visible and celebrated movements, as showcased in their film series on the activists of Otpor in the former Yugoslavia, the leaders of the Orange Revolution demonstrations in Ukraine, and the organizers who helped usher in the downfall of former President Hosni Mubarak during the 2011 Egyptian revolution.

While most other nonviolent INGOs follow a grassroots model of organizational management, these organizations have become increasingly professionalized and embedded in formal international political institutions and networks. Nonviolent Peaceforce (NP), for example, was founded with the support of over two hundred INGOs and nongovernmental organizations (NGOs) in 2002. It has placed unarmed civilian protectors into conflict zones in Iraq, Myanmar, the Philippines, South Sudan, Sudan, Thailand, Ukraine, the United States, and other regions. NP harnesses supporter donations to advance peoples' right to live free from violence perpetrated by other citizens, paramilitaries, and state actors. NP regularly advocates for safe and peaceful resolutions to war and other conflicts between United Nations bodies, the European Union, ASEAN, and other intergovernmental and interstate actors.

Today, nonviolent INGOs like these maintain extensive formal and informal ties throughout the Arab democracy movement, African civil rights and anti-violence movements, human rights initiatives in Latin America, and antiauthoritarian efforts in Asia. Nonviolence has become a global movement with internationally extensive and established professional networks of annual conferences, tactical manuals, seminars, and trainings.

The rapid growth of nonviolent discourse and the expansion of a formalized field of study in the political, civic, and academic arenas has been another powerful force of repertoire globalization. This has played a vital role in infusing a culturally constructed moral order into the repertoire. Discourse drives global moral order frameworks through the articulation of how actors are to be valued and how to interpret and respond to conflicts (Manohka 2009).

From this early era of discourse development through the now global institutionalization of the repertoire, thousands of books have been published on every aspect of nonviolence, many of them celebrating the right ways to engage with conflict of every kind. The Global Books in Print database catalogs over three thousand books on nonviolence that were published in English from the early 1900s through 2010. International news coverage also helps us to understand the deepening institutionalization of nonviolence over time. International news wires covering nonviolent movements and actors increased alongside Gandhi's independence movement in the 1920s, 1930s, and 1940s and picked up again in response to the US civil rights movement in the 1960s. News coverage of nonviolent movements then nearly tripled from the late post-Cold War era into the era of early institutionalization and has continued to grow through the 1990s and 2000s.

Nonviolent studies have also grown into a vibrant interdisciplinary field in the academy, galvanizing a regular exchange between academics and practitioners. There are hundreds of thousands of peer-reviewed articles and scholarly books published on every aspect of nonviolence in fields of history, philosophy, and the social sciences, and hundreds of college and university programs around the world that offer coursework on nonviolence. Some universities have programs solely dedicated to nonviolence studies, while many others fold the topic into peace studies and conflict resolution programs.

The Peace Research Institute, established in Oslo in 1959, has since become a global leader in developing and publishing work on peace studies that often incorporates research on nonviolence. The work of its founder, Johann Galtung, has been formative in extending Gandhian understandings into the analysis of structural peace and systemic violence (Galtung 1969, 1990, 2011b; Galtung and Fisher 2013; Weber 2004). At Indira Gandhi National Open University in India, the largest university in the world, one can gain a post-graduate degree in Gandhian Peace Studies. In June of 2022, the US State Department announced a Gandhi-King scholarly exchange program between the United States and Indian students to build leadership capacity among those studying peace, nonviolence, and conflict resolution.

Furthermore, there are now dozens of international awards and esteemed prizes celebrating organizing, resistance, and leadership in nonviolent movements. The Nobel Peace Prize, one of the most critically acclaimed accolades through which global moral leaders are recognized,[13] has long been awarded to nonviolent visionaries and practitioners. The prize has honored such prominent nonviolence movement leaders as the International Peace Bureau, the American Friends Service, Jane Addams, and Martin Luther King Jr. Recently, the prize has also been used to recognize the work of nonviolence advocates like Adolfo Perez Esquival, Lech Walesa, Aung San Suu Kyi, Wangaari Muta Maatthai, Liu Xiabao, Leymah Gbowee, and Tawakkol Karman. The Nobel model has inspired dozens of international peace prizes that celebrate nonviolent activism, including the International Peace Awards, the Global Peace Awards, the United Nations Human Rights Prize, the UNESCO-Madanjeet Singh Prize for the Promotion of Tolerance and Non-Violence, the Right Livelihood Award, the Gandhi-King Award for Nonviolence, the Ahimsa Award, the Jamnalal Bajaj International Award for Promoting Gandhian Values Outside of India, the El Hibri Peace Award, and the Millennium Peace Prize for Women.

Why Globalization and Institutionalization Matter

Thinking through the examples of conflict presented at the start of this book helps to illuminate why and how globalization and institutionalization matter, how repertoires evolve, and how and why nonviolent movements work in certain contexts.

---

[13] Prior to the world wars, there were already hundreds of "peace societies" throughout Europe. These small societies were dedicated to the idea that citizens should be directly involved in influencing international affairs and that a principal objective of these affairs should be the cessation of violent conflict (Cortright 2008). Inspired by Bertha von Suttner's *Down with Arms*, Alfred Nobel established the Nobel Peace Prize in his will by promising "one part to the person who shall have done the most or the best work for fraternity between nations, the abolition or reduction of standing armies and for the holding and promotion of peace congresses." Von Suttner received the Nobel prize in 1905.

Broadly, globalization and institutionalization create the political context into which movement claims and collective action forms develop, become meaningful, and become effective. Globalization and institutionalization are therefore part of the story of what works and what fails to resonate or shift power. These processes especially matter to nonviolent movements because nonviolence, whether it is adopted as a principled or purely as an instrumental means of resistance, relies so heavily on political context and the cultural foundation of that context in order to work. Nonviolent strategic action scholar George Lakey (1968) suggested that nonviolence succeeds through one of three mechanisms: conversion, convincing one's opponent of the value of change; persuasion, convincing an opponent that it is in their best interest to concede power for other reasons; or coercion, manipulating political or social controls to force concession. But it is important to note that all of these mechanisms rely on the legitimation of nonviolence as part of a modern liberal world order of respect for democracy and democratic entitlements of citizenship in order to work. Tilly argued that repertoires emerge in forms that parallel the governing structure they make claims on. Here, I will demonstrate how broad shifts in global geopolitics can explain the conditions under which nonviolent movements have become not just more prevalent, but also more successful. Additionally, with paradigmatic shifts in global geopolitics on the horizon, it is also important to note where nonviolence may become less effective due to the global repertoire losing the anchors of the modern world polity in which it has emerged.

A global level analysis of the emergence of the nonviolence repertoire over the twentieth century points to the following phenomenal dynamics:

1. The prominence of nonviolent resistance and claims-making is not coincidental but can instead be understood as part of a global movement of resistance methods.
2. While a world polity is in many respects different from a national polity, the general process of iterative national polity formation described by Tilly holds true at the global level. Both repertoire emergence theory and world society theory can help to explain how the expansion of the nonviolence repertoire has been iteratively tied to the globalization of particular political and civic ideals.
3. Nonviolence has globalized as a shared repertoire with common understandings and approaches, but it is not homogenous in practice. The repertoire has also been shaped by distinct interpretations and particular applications. Both religious and secular formulations draw on a common moral order framework legitimating nonviolent resistance as a superior form of claims-making, supporting the humanist ideals foundational to the concept of universal rights.
4. This shared moral order is bolstered by a growing canon of celebrated nonviolence leaders, heroes, and heroines and the moral legitimacy accorded to

nonviolence as a democratic ideal form of resistance. This moral order structure helps to explain how the repertoire often spreads into contexts inhospitable to democratic claims-making.

5. Nonviolence has not been the only collective action repertoire to successfully diffuse in this period – violent methods of collective action have globalized as well.

6. While a local-level lens shows that the success of the nonviolent repertoire may be explained, in part, by savvy strategy at the local level, a macro-level analysis reveals how it may also be understood as broadly contextual, relying on a favorable historical and political context. This lends further support to Tilly's theses on the correspondence between a civic form of political claims-making and the form of polity targeted by those claims, as well as on the relationship between institutionalization and innovation.

7. Institutionalization matters not only to social movements, but also to social movement repertoires, with some important distinctions that merit further scholarly attention.

8. Institutionalization also makes nonviolence more predictable, rendering the technique vulnerable to strategic cooptation and demobilization as well as celebration and adoption decoupled from sincere implementation.

Nonviolence as a Movement of Movements in an Expanding World Polity

As an early biographer of Gandhi noted,

> Such passive resistance methods would not have been successful in the days of Attila the Hun or even of Jaime the Spanish conquistador, who only 700 years ago burned his Majorcan heathen captives in Christian oil. The effectiveness of these methods of the Indian passive resisters today depends upon enlightened public opinion, upon the verdict of a modern world which labels wholesale slaughter of unarmed men as belonging to the days of barbarism, rather than to 1932. Moreover, a new international will to peace had been born from the womb of World War I ... Fifty years ago such a passive resistance movement would not have created a stir. A year before the world war it would probably not have succeeded ... Gandhi took this will to peace and shaped it into a practical political weapon. (Fisher 1932)

Although some version of an international system of nations has existed since the seventeenth century, the basic model of modern state systems as we know it today began to take shape in the eighteenth century (Tilly 1977), spreading rapidly throughout the nineteenth and twentieth centuries. Sociologically, this means the new "verdict of the modern world" and emergence of a "new international will to peace" can be traced to fundamental changes in the structure of the nation-state system (Meyer et al. 1997), the rapid development of intergovernmental and nongovernmental systems into a "third force" in global politics (à la Florini 2000), and the accompanying ethos of entitled citizenship (Soysal 2012). The nonviolence repertoire began to expand more quickly during this period due, in part, to the unprecedented scale of state-making and conflict between nations during the world wars, which left an indelible mark on the model of national sovereignty (Garraty and Gay 1972). At the end of World War II, there were eighty-two sovereign nations in the world. Forty years later, the world had undergone a massive expansion of the system of sovereign nations, largely through decolonization, which has increased the total number of nations to 191 (United Nations 2022). As formerly colonized peoples gained independence, Indigenous movements for statehood sprang up throughout the colonial world.[14] The global delegitimization of colonialism was multidimensional.[15] Following the 1960 signing of the UN Declaration on the Granting of Independence to Colonial Countries and Peoples, the rate of decolonization was six times larger than before (Strang 1990). Throughout these changing times, international actors discussed how best to organize national and global society to favor the form and function of nonviolent movements for independence. The 1960 United Nations Declaration on the Granting of Independence to Colonial Countries and Peoples decreed that,

> All peoples have the right to self-determination; by virtue of that right they freely determine their political status and freely pursue their economic, social and cultural development. ... All armed action or repressive measures of all kinds directed against dependent peoples shall cease in order to enable them to exercise peacefully and freely their right to complete independence, and the integrity of their national territory shall be respected. (United Nations 1960)

Ideals of citizenship favorable to the entitlements of a global nonviolence repertoire have also been written into states' constitutions.[16] In an in-depth

---

[14] This is not to say that shifts in military or economic power are not correlated to some degree with these widespread structural changes. As Strang (1990) points out, a decline in the stature of colonial militaries and a global economic interpenetration that evaporated competition over peripheral markets is also part of the story of decolonization.

[15] Major forces that drove decolonization include a new wave of nationalism, international pressures, and domestic market incentives (Springhall 2001).

[16] Prior to this wave of decolonization, discourse on the relationship between colonizers and colonized peoples communicated a sense of civilizing duties, alongside discussion of preserving economic investments. These sentiments translated into the policy of Western institution building. Foremost among these were educational institutions, which were intended to instill an ideal of what it meant to become "civilized" in Indigenous peoples, providing them a "high road back to Europe" (Chamberlain 1999, 6). This high road was to be constructed through parliamentary

global study of constitutions from 1870 to 1970, Boli (1987) found that state authority can be categorized into three areas of social life: citizens' duties to the state, the state's duties to citizens, and citizens' rights. Following World War II, the constitutional specification of state authority and citizen's rights nearly doubled, while the claims citizens could make of states nearly tripled (Boli 1987). Just as Tilly (1993) pointed to the inclusion of common citizens' claims in Parliament as expanding opportunities for nationally organized repertoires to develop, this general global model of statehood embraces the individual citizen as an equal collaborator in the organization of political life, globally expanding the jurisdiction within which individuals may make claims against the state (Meyer and Jepperson 2000). To this end, national constitutions also increasingly included articles extending citizens' rights to peaceably assemble, free speech, due process, and voting, among a host of other civil, political, social, and economic rights (Boli 1987, 139).

In the early twentieth century, the ideology of human rights came to increasingly permeate new global political units, from intergovernmental organizations (IGOs) and INGOs to states, and in turn shaped how citizenship has been conceived and organized among non-state claimants. A copious number of human rights documents were drafted by various countries and international organizations from the late eighteenth through late nineteenth centuries. These include 113 human rights declarations published between 1863 and 1939 and 666 treaties drafted between 1940 and 2003 (Elliott 2009). In the periods of greatest global political activity among IGO-INGO networks, international bodies conceived of a plethora of new rights to which individual citizens, collectives, and nations should be entitled. In 1949 alone, 117 different rights were declared in international affirmations, while 131 new rights were declared in 1989 and 246 rights were declared in 1990. A total of 1,100 human rights were declared from the 1940s through the 1990s (Elliott 2009). Soysal and colleagues (cf. 2021a and 2021b; 2012) continue to explore new waves of petitions for human rights in the twenty-first century and the changing nature of citizenship in liberal and illiberal regimes as migrants cross borders for a range of reasons.

This expansion of human rights and the efforts of international human rights NGOs have helped enable the globalization of nonviolence. Human rights activists can now rely on the support of third-party interventionists who claim political impartiality on the grounds that they are acting as witnesses in order to

---

politics and federalism, leading colonized people to adopt the culture of the European colonizers (Chamberlain 1999). Even the peripheral former colonies came to be shaped by a Western cultural identity through their national language systems and by constructing Western-style state institutions (Anderson 1983), educational systems (Benavot and Riddle 1998), defense systems (Eyre and Suchman 1996), and scientific and technological ministries (Jang 2003).

deter breeches of the conduct outlined in international law. As an example of this orientation, the founding statement of PBI reads,

> We appeal in particular to ... all those who seek to fulfill the high principles and purposes expressed in the Charter of the United Nations and all who work to preserve human life with dignity, promote human rights, social justice, and self-determination, and to create the conditions of peace. (Peace Brigades International 1981)

This orientation has also been demonstrated through the proliferation of a global organizational structure which has allowed nonviolence organizers to formalize their global efforts. As noted above, INGOs focused on nonviolence and other causes have increased significantly in number. This growth relied upon a preexisting population of general INGOs. There were about 374 known INGOs in 1909. By 1960, there were 1,987 conventional INGOs (Lechner and Boli 2005).[17] The *Yearbook of International Organizations* lists thousands of reciprocal organizing relationships between nonviolent INGOs and other human rights INGOs. Nonviolent Peaceforce, an organization discussed above that places volunteers directly into conflict zones to act as witnesses, deterrers, and mediators of violent conflict, is one prominent example of this network expansion. It is governed by a council of over sixty-five different organizations and is one of many prominent nonviolence INGOs that have consultative status with the United Nations.[18]

The Particularization of a Universal Nonviolence

The history of nonviolence in the long twentieth century also emphasizes the interplay between the repertoire's institutionalization at the global level, whereby more actors subscribe to its general principles and put nonviolence in practice, and at the local level, where, as Tilly noted, innovation occurs incrementally and at the margins. INGOs have been important players in both processes.

As global emissaries of the nonviolence repertoire, it is important to note that nonviolence organizations frequently act as mediators between claims-makers and their targets, states, or other actors (see Sharp 2008). The organizational dimension of international civil society expands the extent to which international "others" may support and spread the repertoire as non-state authorities.

---

[17] The founding of IGOs is highly correlated with those of INGOs. Many IGOs were initially founded as INGOs before being co-opted by states (Boli and Thomas 1999). Because international organizations work with the states which are party to the global treaties they help to develop, these organizations have increasingly acted as a crucial conduit through which global rules are channeled.

[18] The number of general international organizations that have such status has climbed from 250 in 1950 to over 3,000 (Lechner 2009).

Research and advocacy organizations like Human Rights Watch and Amnesty International draw international attention to the repression of nonviolent activists and celebrate their peaceful tactics. Nonviolent scholars and training institutions promote strategic alignment with international third parties to bolster national movement success. And this international diplomacy is multidirectional, initiated by both citizens and states and other governmental bodies. Schock (2005) lists two cases in which international sanctioning pressure was successful: the Philippines and South Africa. Gene Sharp's infamous *From Dictatorship to Democracy* (2002) manual lists seven international forms of diplomatic pressure that can support a nonviolent movement: (1) changes in diplomatic and other representation, (2) delay and cancellation of diplomatic events, (3) withholding of diplomatic representation, (4) severance of diplomatic relations, (5) withdrawal from international organizations, (6) refusal of membership in international bodies, and (7) expulsion from international organizations.[19] Governments can also issue public statements of support, as many countries, including Australia, Botswana, Canada, Eritrea, France, Israel, Kazakhstan, Kyrgyzstan, Malaysia, New Zealand, Russia, Turkey, the United Kingdom, and the United States, did during the Arab Spring (Bryant 2011; Doward 2011; Juppe 2011; McCully 2011; Paxton 2011; Peck 2011; Poonawalla 2011; Ruud 2011). Further, citizens can enlist in "delegations" hosted by INGOs like Christian Peacemaker Teams or Witness for Peace that tour places where nonviolent movements are mobilizing against their states, and in turn pressure their own states to engage in direct advocacy on behalf of those movements. All of these efforts aim to mobilize international political networks to support nonviolent movements by using the repertoire to extend authority to those claimants.

Furthermore, both religious and secular formulations of the repertoire draw on a common moral order framework legitimating nonviolent resistance as a superior form of claims-making. The global repertoire of nonviolence helps to articulate and celebrate the sacred individual in ways analogous to the broader expansion of a liberal world polity. Boli (2006) describes moral order as imbued with ideals of virtue and virtuosity that structure transnational governance through agenda setting as well as through defining the goals and methods for civic and political action. The sacred, Boli explains, construes

---

[19] This is not to suggest that these means always help movements, however. In Nepstad's (2011) recent comparative analysis, she found that in some circumstances the way that sanctions are issued by outside governments can in fact hinder successful mobilization within a country. My point here is to emphasize how the legitimacy of nonviolence as a global repertoire influences states' support for nonviolent movements aimed at regime change in other states, among a host of other issues.

a "framework for distinguishing the laudable from the forbidden" (100). The laudable in the liberal world order is the building up of individual rights and ideals of individual entitlements through a sacred nonviolent community, ideals that undergird nonviolence's core commitments.

Take, for example, some of the lessons drawn from the teachings of Martin Luther King Jr.:

> Nonviolence ... does not seek to defeat or humiliate the opponent, but to win his friendship and understanding ... The end is redemption and reconciliation. The aftermath of nonviolence is the creation of the beloved community. ... The nonviolent attack is directed against forces of evil rather than against persons. ... Nonviolent resistance is a willingness to accept suffering without retaliation. (King 1958)

Reflecting on King's words, Morton (1998) goes on to explain that a system of respect for all is necessary in order to defend the rights of individuals, asserting a dedication to others that demands self-sacrifice through solidarity. In other words, "Try to give to others more than you receive – in any of the infinite number of ways persons can help others" (Morton 1998, 25).

This theme of the sacred mobilized collective runs throughout tactical manuals that emphasize the building of the sacred collective as vital to mobilization. The War Resisters International's 1991 edited volume on social defense puts forth that "social defence implies a degree of unity, or consensus, on the part of the civilian population." The goal of social defense is described not merely as the preservation of any one individual's threatened rights – as the author notes, "organising means building community." These sentiments hearken back to Gandhi's conceptualization of nonviolence as building mutuality, expanding equality, and diffusing freedom:

> To me it is self-evident that if freedom is to be shared by all – even physically the weakest, the lame, and the halt – they must be able to contribute an equal share in its defense. How that can be possible when reliance is placed on armaments, my plebian mind fails to understand. I therefore swear and shall continue to swear by non-violence, i.e., by satyagraha or soul force. In its physical incapacity is no handicap, and even a frail woman or child can pit herself or himself on equal terms against a giant armed with the most powerful weapons. (Gandhi 1946)

One Witness for Peace's reflection asserts that "the deeper we go, the more connected we become." This is written of short-term delegations that have traveled together and of the connections Witness for Peace delegations have built with Central America, as also of the connections between global political problems and the broader nonviolence movement.

Evidence of the sacred collective as a driving force of the nonviolence repertoire also runs throughout assessments and case histories of global activists' work to support local movements. This is articulated in the International Fellowship for Reconciliation's narrative of its role in the Philippines democracy movement:

> How can one kneel and stare down rumbling tanks and hundreds of soldiers trained for military battle, especially when all one has is supplies of food to offer, words for conversion, faith and hope in their common humanity, and prayer to the possible source of that humanity and power? (Sasaran 2006)

Sasaran goes on to explain how the Filipino concept of nonviolence, *alay dangal*, means "to offer dignity" realized through collective action and interests:

> They [IFOR, the Catholic Church, and other mobilizing civil society organizations] taught that human dignity was an unalterable, inextinguishable, and equivalent value given (i.e. inherent) to each human. Regardless of what we have, such as money, power, intelligence, looks, etc., or what we do, such as generosity, justice, murder, sin, etc., human dignity remains unaltered, inextinguishable, and equal for each human. We are encouraged and perhaps drawn by gratitude to both illuminate and live in accord with this gift of dignity in all people by our choices. (Sasaran 2006)

She concludes by underlining the universalizing notion of nonviolence as a collectivizing force that can work across the lines of conflict as well as national and cultural borders:

> Yet, the people of the Philippines were largely experiencing economic and political oppression, which ignored their dignity and left the oppressors living in discord with their own dignity. Thus, from the perspective of *alay dangal*, "to offer dignity," both groups were suffering and as a community were in need of restoring their sense of human dignity. The power of nonviolence activates this restorative and liberating process. (Sasaran 2006)

Finally, to enshrine the laudable in the global moral order, there exists a host of moral guardians, activists, and entrepreneurs who discuss and elaborate on sacred entities' vulnerabilities and protection needs, rights, and justified expectations (Boli 2006). In a global moral order, there is an easily identifiable canon of moral authorities who appropriately exhibit "moral displays" and are regularly celebrated for practicing moral ideals of right behavior. They are identified and applauded through informal descriptions of saintliness as well as through formal means of celebration, including internationally recognized awards. We see this celebration in action in a forward to a comparative study of nonviolent resistance in Latin America written by Boff (1991), one of the earliest and most well-known liberation theologians:

> This answer [of active nonviolence] is inspired in part by the extraordinary example of persons who have successfully demonstrated another way of confronting highly conflictive situations. Some of the best known are Mahatma Gandhi, Martin Luther King Jr., Dom Hélder Câmara, and Adolfo Perez Esquival. (Boff 1991, vii)

It is therefore notable that this moral order is sanctified by a growing canon of celebrated repertoire leaders and heroes and heroines. Boli (2006) explains that because leaders like Gandhi and King have become aligned with the sacred, the lives they have lived stand as exemplars to be followed. "Righteousness is demonstrated by opposing oppression (Amnesty International), fighting inequality (Gandhi, Mandela), preserving life (Mèdecins Sans Frontières), protecting persecuted groups (Martin Luther King Jr., Dalai Lama), and so on" (Boli 2006, 10–11). Such righteousness is also evident in secularists' descriptions of the repertoire. Jack DuVall, a founding director of the International Center for Nonviolent Conflict, refers to St. Paul and former US President Jimmy Carter in his call to defend the sacralization of nonviolence in supporting democracy:

> Just as St. Paul understood that his freedom was God-given, a natural right, the world is coming to acknowledge that rights are not conferred by states – they must be honored by states because they belong to individuals. Eventually it will be accepted everywhere that each person's rights come before any ruler's will and that no government is legitimate unless it is based on the people's consent.
>
> The day when that becomes a universal fact will not arrive until the world realizes that rights are won more surely by the people than by terrorists or armies. To make nonviolent struggle the global boulevard to political liberation, we must relentlessly propagate the ideas and strategies that pave its way to victory. Former President Jimmy Carter has said that "nonviolent valor can end oppression." But not until we all enlist to help the valiant. (DuVall 2004)

The give and take between the globalization of common forms of action and celebrated practices and the local innovation of unique understandings and applications of nonviolence has also sometimes occurred alongside contention and fragmentation. Following from the ideals of universal human rights and the sovereignty of nations as well as the ideals of democratic participatory process, many nonviolence advocates strongly emphasize local and Indigenous agency and distinct cultural contributions to the repertoire. Robertson (1992) noted this dynamic as integral to the process of cultural globalization that both unfolded into a "particularization of universal" ideals and brought about a "universalization of particular" frameworks related to nonviolence.

It is therefore important to note that while globalization affects the spread and adoption of common frameworks of meaning and action, it does not necessarily result in the homogenization of social movements or other political and cultural forms. That the repertoire is easily understood to encompass distinct conceptual approaches as part of its global cache – including alay dangal, *ubuntu*, and firmenza permanente, among others – illustrates this point. The global diffusion of nonviolence has followed multiple paths, resulting in diverse outcomes. The third-party witness organization Christian Peacemaker Teams (CPT), for example, provided nonviolence support to local Iraqis in response to the US invasion in 2003. In late 2005, several CPT members were taken hostage, including Tom Fox, a lifelong devoted Quaker and pacifist who was later executed. During the time CPT was on the ground in Iraq, it had gained such regard among locals that they were able to collect data for a Human Rights Watch condition report. Following Fox's death, CPT moved out of Iraq, transferring some witness volunteers to other countries. Despite this very serious setback, after CPT departed, there was an initiative in Iraq to establish a Muslim Peacemaker Team, a particularization of this now universalizing repertoire. This is one possible outcome for the expansion of a collective action repertoire being practiced in the context of a national polity (in this case one defined by foreign military intervention and violent fundamentalism as well as movement forces).

Nonviolence as a global repertoire has also evolved through internal disputes among practitioners and advocates over how best to articulate and apply the approach. DuVall's many contributions to the repertoire as a director at ICNC represent part of a longer effort to secularize nonviolence into an amoral system for realizing democratic social justice. Gene Sharp was among the earliest scholars to make a move toward a secular theory of nonviolence. In his 1960 *Gandhi Wields the Weapon of Moral Power*, an exploration of three case studies of nonviolent movements published when he was under the tutelage of peace scholars Arne Naess and Johan Galtung, Sharp explored Gandhi's morally infused approach to this process. Sharp's framework of nonviolence shifted, however, as he began to work with funding from the US Department of Defense. By the time he published *The Politics of Nonviolent Action* in 1973, his three volume, nine hundred page tome on the power, methods, and dynamics of nonviolent action, Sharp had transformed Richard Gregg's concept of "moral jiu jitsu," the process through which activists may disarm their opponents by tapping into their moral worldview in unexpected ways, into a secularized "political jiu jitsu." His later works delved into nonviolent modeling of military and defense strategies.

This internal tension continues within the repertoire today. Ackerman of ICNC asserts, for example, that "nonviolent sanctions have most often been used by people who needed to make practical choices under very difficult circumstances, rather than by people committed to the avoidance of bloodshed for ethical reasons" (Ackerman and Kruegler 1994, 5). Following in this line of thinking, some scholars in political science and sociology have moved away from the term "nonviolence" due to its moralist philosophical sentiments. In its place, they have embraced the more clinical concept of "nonviolent civil resistance."[20] The International Center for Nonviolent Conflict explains this new normative distinction in the following manner:

> "Nonviolence" is usually a moral choice. Nonviolent conflict is usually a pragmatic choice. Nonviolent conflict is about power – organizing and applying it to fight for and win rights or other political, economic, or social goals. Many people that have used nonviolent action in the past wanted to advance their rights or interests but chose nonviolent methods either because they saw that violence had been ineffective in the past or because they had no violent weapons at their disposal. (ICNC 2016)

This assertion emphasizes the tension intrinsic to the particularization of the universal through the spread of world culture. World society provides a common framework, but global movements can also deepen many forms of resistance and antagonism as conflicting interpretations of that framework unfold (Lechner and Boli 2005, 15). A broad institutional context may foment diametrically oppositional movements (Roy 2004; Kurzman 2004). This is also found in the broader cultural proliferation of post-World War II human rights that have evolved into contradictory interpretations of entitlements and obligations (Meyer et al. 1997; Frank and Meyer 2002), especially as older institutions generate new orientations in response to new cultural frameworks (Casanova 1994).

It also underscores the particularity and oversights of rational-choice (i.e. Western and individualist) understandings of people's behavior, a theoretical elaboration that has predominated in nonviolent civil resistance studies. This perspective recognizes only one form of power-over politics that characterizes some, but certainly not all, movements committed to nonviolence (Gallo-Cruz 2021a). Rational-choice theories ignore the value-laden commitments even of other secular movement leaders (McGuinness 1998) who may hold to moral goals of "bringing down the dictator" (York 2002) while perpetuating other forms of oppression such as ethnic hatred, sexism, and homophobia (Fridman 2011). It also masks the moral order fibers of a purportedly value-neutral form of practical nonviolence that is intrinsically bound to particular cultural and political systems, such as elite-led neoliberal economies where questions of

---

[20] Lambelet (2021) has cogently argued that this move can be understood to stem in part from a reinterpretation of Weber's distinction between principled and pragmatic forms of action, allowing for secular and sacred affiliations to be counted in the expanding canon of case studies.

political rights factor into moral discussions but questions of structural inequality often do not (Chabot and Sharifi 2013; Smith 2019a). Nonetheless, recognizing that nonviolence can become decoupled from moral and ethical motivations is important too. Terrorist and illicit criminal organizations, for example, may sometimes employ nonviolent methods simply because they can or do so strategically to capitalize on the public legitimacy those tactics may afford them (Mandić 2021).

Scripts and Strategies

Although there is strong evidence for Tillyian and world polity theory assertions about repertoire scripts and learning informing the patterning of strategic choices, it is important to acknowledge that other actions are always possible. A long historical perspective shows that the institutionalization, resources, and learning of violent kinds of claims-making have been successful as well.

The same era that saw the rapid systematization and expansion of nonviolence and the decolonization of dozens of new sovereign states was also marked by high levels of internal violence. While the global scale of the conflict between national militaries during the world wars remains unique, the postwar period has seen an exceptional surge in violent civil wars. In rushing to prop up fledgling states through postwar initiatives for universal national sovereignty, the international community left impoverished, weak nations to fight out new and existing conflicts within their newly imposed borders. In some cases, international intervention has also further inflamed power differentials between favored elites and other citizens by exacerbating local weaknesses and tensions. From 1945 to 1997 there was an estimated 165 percent increase in the incidence of violent civil wars worldwide (Hironaka 2008). At times, these conflicts have occurred at a rate exceeding ten times the historical average, with some dragging on upward of twenty years (Hironaka 2008; Sarkees and Schafer 2000). These conflicts have wreaked widespread, lasting devastation on postcolonial nations. Furthermore, regional security interests, still realized through military power, lacked effective conflict-resolution strategies. This marked the latter twentieth century as an "age of global conflict" (Held et al. 1999). It is remarkable and significant that the decades in which nonviolence has been most actively globalized have also been some of the most violent (Brecke 2012). This has been due in part to the violent mobilization of many nationalist movements (Dandeker 1998; Rupesinghe and Rubio 1994).

Additionally, the first Cold War ushered in an arms race of historic proportions. Twentieth century technology developed for warfare has been unique in that it promotes new, totalizing forms of destruction by involving whole societies in producing weaponry that target large numbers of people, such as warplanes, nuclear bombs, and poison gas (Edgarton 2007). Military spending continues to increase, with the world's total spending nearing 2 trillion in 2019 (Szmigiera 2021). While many of these smaller scale conflicts have served as ongoing proxy wars between global powers (Berman and Lake 2019; Innes 2012), the 2022 Russian invasion of Ukraine and China's efforts to annex Taiwan – both of which were presented as efforts to reclaim lost territory and stave off the encroachment of Western military powers along the borders of sovereign nations – have moved pundits to declare a new Cold War (Engle 2014; Kalb 2015).

The same global forces and structures that have supported the globalization of nonviolence, including international organizational networks, have also contributed to the spread of violence and terrorism. The list of IGOs dedicated to controlling arms and arms treaties is extensive. International agreements have generated a number of new ways for non-state actors to regulate the use of military intervention and violent conflict across borders (Devetak and Hughes 2008). The volume of international arms transfers grew significantly in the post-Cold War period, peaking in 1982 before beginning to increase again in 2005 (Holtom and Bromley 2010). The bulk of these weapons transfers are made from a handful of wealthy nations to developing nations (Conventional Arms Transfer 2018), though advances in global technology and commerce have also enabled the informal distribution of arms and other violent weaponry to insurgents the world over (Louise 1995). The UIA lists numerous INGOs that claim they are making global peace through terrorist methods. Scholars have also demonstrated how terrorism has diffused through global conceptualization and organization (LaFree, Xie, and Matanock 2018; Polo 2020).

These findings broaden the perspective on what makes nonviolent movements successful, reiterating a central point of all sociology: context matters. The scripts and strategies devised by claims-makers emerge in a particular context, through social learning, and in conversation with the actions and responses of targets. A historical examination of the diffusion of nonviolent campaigns challenges the political science thesis that tactics matter more to movement development than globalization. When one reexamines nonviolent movements in the context of their historical development through different qualitative waves of global repertoire expansion, the success of these movements is shown to have increased in line with the global institutionalization of the repertoire's networks and authority, but this has occurred alongside competing scripts.

A historical reassessment of one of the most highly cited and influential recent studies of nonviolent campaign success helps to illustrate this point. In a 2011 article in *International Security* and a subsequent book entitled *Why*

Civil Resistance Works: The Strategic Logic of Nonviolent Conflict, Stephan and Chenoweth use panel analysis to compare violent and nonviolent resistance campaigns in order to identify which campaigns were more successful and why. In the first version of their Nonviolent and Violent Campaigns and Outcomes (NAVCO) database, they examined 100 nonviolent campaigns and 209 violent campaigns carried out from 1900 to 2006. The updated NAVCO 2.0 (Chenoweth and Lewis 2013) provides new information on 100 nonviolent and 150 violent campaigns from 1945 to 2006.[21] What these researchers found was that over 53 percent of nonviolent campaigns achieved success as compared to violent campaigns, of which only 26 percent achieved success. Their analysis emphasizes the importance of the global structural features I discussed above, namely the effects of international support in the form of sanctions (which was found to be insignificant for nonviolent campaigns but significant for violent campaigns) and foreign state support (which was found to be somewhat helpful to nonviolent campaigns and more so for violent campaigns).

By reanalyzing both NAVCO datasets through the historical lens, outlined in Tables 1 and 2, I have also found that these nonviolent campaigns continued to diffuse despite higher failure rates in the 1940s through the 1970s and, as I have argued here, through a favorable intersection of globalizing forces. Formal organizations acted as cultural entrepreneurs, the world system praised the repertoire as the best route toward democracy (even though NAVCO shows them to be less successful in these earlier eras), and a vibrant popular and academic discourse celebrated nonviolence as the means to realize universal human rights. To be clear, this reassessment does not negate the findings that two principal factors explain nonviolence's greater likelihood of success: that nonviolent movements garner more support both within states and among international allies through a more legitimate approach and that the violent repression of peaceful movements is more likely to backfire against violent regimes. Rather, a global historical perspective on this data suggests that the nonviolent campaigns did not become more likely to succeed than violent ones *until* the era of institutionalization, driven in part by the concerted international organization and the

---

[21] From the NAVCO website: "Whereas NAVCO 1.0 focused on the campaign, NAVCO 2.0 focuses on the campaign-year. It contains yearly data on 250 nonviolent and violent insurrections between 1945 and 2006 (100 nonviolent, 150 violent). These campaigns constitute the full population of known cases between 1945 and 2006 that held 'maximalist' goals of overthrowing the existing regime, expelling foreign occupations, or achieving self-determination at some point during the campaign. NAVCO 2.0 also expands data on campaign strategy, organization, and internal dynamics. For example, it reports the number of participating organizations, political goals, leadership structure, demographic composition, and tactical strategies, such as the building of parallel institutions and use of communications."

Tables 1 and 2 A Historical Assessment of the NAVCO datasets (Chenoweth 2019; Chenoweth and Lewis 2013) shows the development of successful and unsuccessful violent and nonviolent campaigns across distinct historical waves of repertoire emergence. Nonviolence continued to evolve as a global repertoire despite being less successful in earlier eras. Only when it reached a significant level of global institutionalization coinciding with the fall of the Eastern Bloc, did nonviolent campaigns begin to experience greater success.

Campaign success from NAVCO 1.0

	Successful Violent	Successful Nonviolent
Early Conceptualization Period, through 1944	7 (3%)	4 (4%)
Post-world war Systematization Period, 1945–1979	26 (12%)	9 (9%)
Early Institutionalization Period, 1980–1989	5 (2%)	17 (17%)
High Institutionalization 1990–2000s	13 (6%)	26 (26%)

Campaign success from NAVCO 2.0

	Successful Violent	Successful Nonviolent
Post World War Systematization, 1945–1979	28 (25%)	11 (10%)
Early Institutionalization Period, 1980–1989	5 (4%)	15 (13%)
High Institutionalization 1990–2000s	12 (11%)	41 (37%)

building up of a global repertoire of discourse, practice, and favorable political structures for nonviolence in the 1980s, with the greatest cluster of successful campaigns identified by NAVCO occurring around the fall of the Eastern bloc, an era in which world powers historically opposed to the entitlements claimed by nonviolent movements were in the process of receding. That success came at a time when the Cold War was coming to a close makes the corresponding groundswell of new independence movements pushing out already failing former communist states a predictable outcome rather than a paradoxical one. We might therefore reconsider the success rate in these particular studies as a measure of the effect of the fall of the Eastern Bloc, which, for better or for worse, welcomed in new political rights alongside new neoliberal economic policies, on independence movements.

It is important to weigh these points when considering why the success of modern nonviolent campaigns is currently in decline or, to take a longer historical view, why it peaked around the era of the fall of the Eastern Bloc and the decades after. Scholars now contemplate how nonviolence will fare in the face of a new wave of authoritarianism (Chenoweth 2021; Cebul and Pinckney 2022; Zunes 2022). In her recent work, Chenoweth (2022) notes that the power of nonviolence is waning in some contexts. I would argue that it has always been context dependent, a difference of analytical perspective by which we arrive at similar empirical but distinct theoretical points. This so-called retreat of the era of nonviolence's success, whether one views it as an immediate change or a long-term fluctuation, may play out through the soft dominance of neoliberal market power (Chabot and Sharifi 2013; Pinckney 2020; Smith 2019a), the hard power of dominant economic nations propping up military operations in peripheral states (Kuppuswamy 2011; Reilly 2013), or through a surge in populist movements supporting autocratic rulers (de la Torre and Peruzzotti 2018; Mietzner 2020a, 2020b; Sombatpoonsiri 2019).

It is therefore important to note that context is key to both diffusion and success. This is not a new insight to those who have contemplated nonviolence's distinct outcomes. Many have written on the dangers of blanket assumptions that nonviolence will always or even often be successful (cf. Davies 2014; Gelderloos 2013; Nepstad 2011). David Meyer (2019) has recently made the point that focusing primarily on the effectiveness of nonviolent tactics at the expense of larger contexts leads researchers to miss larger effects. He recognizes the sense of moral courage that can be evoked by stories of solitary acts of nonviolence in the face of powerful systems while also urging social movements scholars to expand the frame of analysis so that the long run-up to and long-term effects of collective action can be more fully understood (see also Case 2021).

Research on the international context shaping revolutions also emphasizes this point. Daniel Ritter's (2014) *The Iron Cage of Liberalism* takes seriously the interlocking of culture and global political opportunity for movements in Iran, Tunisia, and Egypt. Lawson's (2019) *Anatomy of Revolution* explains how other revolutions have been ushered in a phenomenal historical wave of 'decolonization' in the twentieth century. Lawson explains that the very concept of revolutionary emancipation and the general form of what is understood and practiced as revolutionary has a historical and sociocultural origin story. Lawson has also argued that revolutionary forms are at once universalizable and yet particular in practice.

In *Civil Resistance and Nonviolence*, contemporary Mexican nonviolence organizer Pietro Ameglio explains how and why the repertoire works in the context of a twenty-first century nation-state:

> This form of nonviolent struggle is based on the principle that governments socially depend on collaboration and anticipated blind obedience to authority to be able to execute all forms of punishment that it demands of us, as well as the loyalty of the Armed Forces and police, without questioning the inhumanity of its orders on several occasions. (Ameglio 2010, 102)

Ameglio goes on to elaborate that it is when these civic-political understandings shift, opportunities for nonviolent "people-power" emerge.

But what if those understandings never take hold in the first place? Or what if they shift toward authoritarianism? What if they take on a two-sided character and shift discursively toward democracy but economically and structurally toward a greater polarization of power? From the perspective of repertoire emergence and contentious performance studies, the repertoire may be expected to fail where the targeted nation-state, industry, or other repressive targets resist the principles of democratic statehood, citizenship, and entitlements upon which the nonviolence repertoire is based.

In Conclusion

As a citizen in 2023, a time riven with new wars and new nuclear threats, new kinds and levels of everyday violence, new forms of weaponry, and new predictions for violence in the years to come, I would much prefer to live in the society of peaceful possibilities articulated by both the secular and moralist iterations of the nonviolence repertoire. My purpose in undertaking this study is not to refute the beauty, the justice, or the moral integrity of nonviolence and its practitioners, all of which I honor and admire greatly on a personal level. Rather, my intention has been motivated by a profound sociological curiosity to better understand how this impressively well-networked movement of movements that has so phenomenally reshaped the way the world has come to understand and practice resistance. In the years since I began this research, the field of nonviolent studies has grown exponentially to offer new formulas and findings for further uplifting the movement for peace and democracy around the world. But these studies often miss one of the most fundamental points about how claims-making repertoires work: repertoires are social creations that correspond to particular kinds of institutions and particular historical developments, and they rely on these conditions to work well or to work at all.

When early scholars began to disentangle the mechanics of what makes nonviolence work, they identified many elements crucial to its success. These include those contained in Gregg's concept of "moral jiu jitsu," maneuvers that can resonate with a ruling moral order (whether or not individuals prescribe to the moral order is less important than how it governs political legitimacy and authority) and the element of surprise, through which targets are left unprepared to repress movements. Sharp's revision of the concept supplanted the moral with the political but acknowledged a similar reliance on movements' resonance within a favorable system. In this tradition, a political "power over" could be waged through political pressure or economic pressure, which is why, of the three principal techniques Sharp gives attention to, protest, intervention, and noncooperation, the latter has historically proven to be the most effective in shifting power from below (most notably through general strikes). But these conclusions belie some additional necessary conditions for these efforts to be successful. Principally, these include:

1. vulnerability to moral or political claims or economic changes;
2. a principal orientation to some dimension of the common social system in which claims are anchored; and
3. the establishment of a clear boundary across which conflict is waged so that disagreements in political power must be confronted.

Each of these social forces can be seen in the historical and qualitative assessment I have provided above.

From within the world of nonviolence, there are a number of strategic considerations to be made regarding how movements can (nonviolently) capitalize on the vulnerability of their targets, whether it is through social methods of negotiation and persuasion or political and economic maneuvers of coercion. At the level of strategizing, one might consider the ethics, and mechanisms for efficacy that will work with different targets. A macro-level approach to the repertoire reveals that vulnerabilities exist because targets are in some ways beholden to the systems movements have access to, whether those systemic constraints are moral or material. Thus, these elements can be understood from a different perspective of what shapes success. Understanding takes on more nuance when considering the socially constructed nature of conflictual fields and conflicts.

People Power for Whom and for What?

There are two oversights scholars can easily make by not taking this macro-level view. The first I have discussed through an in-depth theoretical consideration of the kinds of movements that fall outside the purview of Sharpian and political science approaches to nonviolent people power (Gallo-Cruz 2021a; see also McGuiness 1993). This involves a strong understanding that not all actors want mobility in the systems dominated by targets nor do all movements desire the elimination of targets' power. Many work to create new social possibilities outside these systems. There is a fundamental difference between power-over studies and power-over conflicts and power-to movements, to put it succinctly (Gallo-Cruz 2021a). This does not negate the repertoire's global legitimacy; rather, it underscores its place among many possibilities for meaning and practice.

Meyer and Jepperson (2000) explain the fundamental shift that occurred in the post-World War era, noting that new kinds of understandings about actors and their agency impelled profound global forms of action and organization through which individuals have increasingly and legitimately come to expect and demand a host of new entitlements and rights from states. These expectations are often decoupled from practice on the ground, though, as systems of stratification remain entrenched around the world, rendering women, racial and ethnic minorities, sexual minorities, members of different religious faiths, people of different economic and cultural classes, and, to different degrees, children, disabled people, and the elderly relegated to de facto disadvantaged lives. The point of repertoire emergence and world society theories, however, is not to quantify the difference in outcomes but to trace the effects of common orientations. Each of the above-mentioned groups has engaged with nonviolence as a means of redressing their grievances and making claims. Still, it is an oversight of nonviolent studies, which has not yet given critical consideration to the repertoire as a global cultural construction, that real conflicts between the ideals celebrated in the repertoire and the values of systems put forth in its engagement persist, with internal contradictions in values that can be diametrically opposed. There exists at once a particular cultural content and a specific structural orientation of the repertoire. These inform the distinct ethics, audiences, ways of conceptualizing goals and measuring efficacy, and the selected targets of nonviolent claims-making. The contentious performances that global nonviolence makes possible have been increasingly generally patterned over time and across a personable network of emissaries and activist organizations, but they are also always specified in their expression.

In a recent series of critical essays, Smith (2019a, 2019b) made the point that Sharpian visions for revolutionary transition often amount to a new concentration of power in the hands of those who benefit from neoliberal, albeit democratically elected, regimes. She also made the assertion that Sharp's now global program for nonviolent action had forwarded a US-oriented Cold War defense strategy through the framework of nonviolence. In response, Smith was charged with "getting Gene Sharp wrong" on his choices regarding strategy and leadership, though this criticism side-stepped her deeper concerns about how elected leaders can create new structural inequalities by commandeering these movements, even as her critics agree that preparation for what comes after the fall of the dictator is essential (Lakey 2019). And while nonviolence peace scholar Galtung (1969) is most often cited for the innovative concept of "structural peace," those social structural features of society that allow all citizens to realize wellbeing, neoliberal forms of democratic governance significantly rely on the unseen forms of violence and harm intrinsic to an extractive industrial economy (Shapiro and McNeish 2021).

Furthermore, the phenomenon of persistent unequal systems takes on a new dimension when values and status differences intersect. How actors, power-holders, targets of resistance, and resistance movements view others in a political or social field can be completely at odds with how they view themselves as well as their goals. These inconsistencies often contribute to the eruption of conflict in the first place but can also render those actors irrelevant or invisible to political processes or conflicts, even when nonviolence is a guiding repertoire for collective action (see Gallo-Cruz 2021b).

Institutionalization as an Opportunity for Cooptation and Demobilization

The second oversight regards the opportunities targets now have to co-opt and capture movements through discourse that aligns with resisters' goals but which is not sincerely in line with targets' intentions. I have documented how, for example, the discourse surrounding the movement to close the US Army School of the Americas has been co-opted by the Western Hemisphere Institute for Security and Cooperation (WHINSEC), a newly reengineered protest-resistance institution (Gallo-Cruz 2012; Gallo-Cruz 2015). Targets like WHINSEC may adopt a counter-framing of their policies and position that positively embraces the ideals championed by movements, making it difficult for these movements to gain traction. These fuzzy forms of demobilization are further enabled by an increasingly powerful and savvy global public relations industry. There are currently more people employed in the public relations industry than in journalism and the field boasts an incredible economic resource base and expanding political connections (Navarro 2023). Furthermore, as I learned from one Palestinian organizer, governments have long studied the principles of nonviolent mobilization to gain strategic advantage in preventing movements' from seizing power. He recounted how shocked he was to learn that Gene Sharp himself accepted an invitation from the Israeli Defense Force to teach his techniques following the success of nonviolence in mobilizing the *intifada*.

Recent research by Guriev and Treisman (2022) in *Spin Dictators: The Changing Face of Tyranny in the 21st Century* cogently makes the point that authoritarian leaders can now more easily use covert methods of information control to garner sympathy and support among the public. Eco-activist and farmers' advocate Shiva (2022) recounts that during her early work on the Chipko movement in India she had been puzzled at why so many rural citizens who depended on the land were planting Eucalyptus trees instead of growing food. Then, she "found the World Bank hiding behind newly planted Eucalyptus trees," explaining how she learned that the World Bank had co-opted the sustainability language of the Chipko forest protectors and offered green grants to plant Eucalyptus trees that would later be harvested by the paper industry. This cooptation is well understood among scholars who document the use of public relations to undermine environmental movements (Aronczyk and Espinoza 2021; Brulle and Werthman 2021; Oreskes and Conway 2010) and the growing field of studies about public relations and politics documenting too many other examples to list here. Along with government and military regimes and intergovernmental organizations, targeted industries systematically study strategic collective action to develop more effective counter-framing and demobilization strategies.

However, while social movements scholars have long understood that institutionalization alters the path of mobilization, much less attention has been given to tracing the ways in which co-optation and demobilization occurs, stifling the long-term success of movements. Even in the field of nonviolent studies, which includes examining the staying power of democracy after nonviolent uprisings, much less attention is given to the substantive alignment between movement aspirations and political transformations (though see Kadivar 2022).

What movement scholars have written about institutionalization is that it can help to ensure political survival and formalize the influence of movements, but it may also mark the end of the "sense of unlimited possibility" generated earlier in a movement's development (Meyer and Tarrow 1998). Because citizen protests are now a normal and legitimate part of the political process in many states, targets can expect routinized, predictable repertoires of contention that may have diminishing impacts (McCarthy and McPhail 1998) as targets can also develop defensive strategic responses to head off the disruptive potential of social movements (Kubik 1998). In states where open protests are more novel, on the other hand, nonviolence is more likely to result in outright repression. Global and local brokers of nonviolence may therefore struggle with the challenge of negotiating new international directives in conflicts with entrenched opposition, ingrained proclivities, and strained capacities (Chua 2018; Cole 2020; Levitt and Merry 2009; Merry 2006).

At a global level of analysis, it is important to note how, as Tilly described it, the institutionalization of movement forms diffuses across an uneven geopolitical and sociocultural global terrain. This is evident in several ways. There is both a "pattern" to how social movements repeatedly utilize tactics and an "order" to how these tactics are conceptualized as important to claims-making (à la Jepperson 1991; Zucker 1987). Movements, like other major social transformations in organizational fields, are often spearheaded and mobilized by visionaries or cultural entrepreneurs. Therefore, in studying the institutionalization of social movements, we uncover a dynamism between path dependence and transformation (à la Jepperson 1991; Zucker 1987). This area of research has also not yet been given adequate attention in world polity and globalization scholarship. Although the ceremonious adoption of global norms constitutes a central tenet of world society frameworks, the ways in which those ideals are spread through tactical repertoires that can be adopted, co-opted, and reengineered by resistance movements and counter resistance efforts have not been carefully explored in ways that may challenge the framework's understanding of decoupling and the political impacts of legitimation. This phenomenon is an important element on the current global political stage and is relevant to work on fragmentation and the paradoxical role anti-globalization efforts have played in the development of global politics. Likewise, it will be difficult for scholars normatively devoted to proving nonviolence more successful in all contexts to adequately understand the limits to success posed by institutionalization. But there are many arenas in which conflicts continue to unfold and nonviolent protest has proven unsuccessful time and again. The examples mentioned at the start of this monograph are classic cases which underscore this paradox.

It is my hope that more scholarship and social movement strategic thinking will move away from romanticized visions of transformation within the liberal order and pay greater attention to the systemic injustices that can be discursively swept under the rug through engagements with nonviolent (and other) social movements. Understanding the nature of the institutionalization of a collective action repertoire is important, therefore, not only for understanding its historical and global context – institutionalization also leads movements to become more predictable in their approach and thus easier to defeat. Internal contradictions between the nonviolence movement's global orientation and its support for Indigenous agency and knowledge represent both a strength and a weakness for the repertoire. On the one hand, this duality can provide a path to repertoire transformation and renewal that strengthens global bonds and broadens strategic and tactical diversity. On the other hand, it can be co-opted by targets who charge third parties providing activist support and solidarity to local movements with perpetuating patrimonial interference in sovereign states' affairs. In an impending new world order shaped by shifting global political economic positions among world powers, where and how nonviolence will continue to spread and be effective remains to be fully understood. This can be said of many kinds of general claims-making techniques and political models for action that global scholars have long concerned themselves with, however. Future scholarship should broaden the perspective on global movements and social change by asking new questions about the history, nature, and limits of nonviolence in ongoing conflicts.

References

Ackerman, Peter, and Christopher Kruegler. 1994. *Strategic Nonviolent Conflict: The Dynamics of People Power in the Twentieth Century.* Westport, CT: Praeger.

Alasuutari, Pertti, and Ali Qadir. 2019. *Epistemic Governance: Social Change in the Modern World.* Cham, CH: Springer International.

Ameglio, Pietro. 2010. "Civil Resistance and Nonviolence." In *International Security: Peace, Development and Environment-Vol. II*, edited by Ursula Oswald Spring, 164–173. Oxford, United Kingdom: UNESCO-EOLSS.

Amro, Issa, and Zak Witus. 2021. "It's Time for Jews to Join Palestinians in Civil Resistance to the Occupation." *Forward*, August 11, 2021. https://forward.com/opinion/474065/its-time-for-jews-to-join-with-palestinians-in-incivil-resistance.

Anderson, Benedict. 1983. *Imagined Communities.* London: Verso.

Andrews, Kenneth T., and Michael Biggs. 2006. "The Dynamics of Protest Diffusion: Movement Organizations, Social Networks, and News Media in the 1960 Sit-Ins." *American Sociological Review* 71, no. 5 (October): 752–777. https://doi.org/10.1177/000312240607100503.

Anisin, Alexei. 2020. "Debunking the Myths behind Nonviolent Civil Resistance." *Critical Sociology* 46, no. 7–8 (November): 1121–1139. https://doi.org/10.1177/0896920520913982.

Aronczyk, Melissa, and Maria I. Espinoza. 2021. *A Strategic Nature: Public Relations and the Politics of American Environmentalism.* Oxford: Oxford University Press.

Ash, Timothy. 2009. "A Century of Civil Resistance: Some Lessons and Questions." In *Civil Resistance and Power Politics: The Experience of Nonviolent Action from Gandhi to the Present*, edited by Robert Adams and Timothy Garton Ash, 371–392. Oxford: Oxford University Press.

Banks, Arthur S., and Kenneth A. Wilson 2022. "Cross-National Time-Series Data (CNTS)." *Databanks International.* Jerusalem, Israel. Accessed January 25, 2019. www.cntsdata.com.

Barrett, Deborah, and Charles Kurzman. 2004. "Globalizing Social Movement Theory: The Case of Eugenics." *Theory and Society* 33: 487–527. https://doi.org/10.1023/B%3ARYSO.0000045719.45687.AA.

Beales, A. C. F. 1931. *The History of Peace; a Short Account of the Organised Movements for International Peace.* New York: The Dial Press.

Beck, Sanderson. 2008. *South Asia 1800–1950: Ethics of Civilization.* Goleta, CA: World Peace Communications.

Beckfield, Jason. 2003. "Inequality in the World Polity: The Structure of International Organization." *American Sociological Review* 68, no. 3 (June): 401–424. https://doi.org/10.2307/1519730.

Beckfield, Jason. 2010. "The Social Structure of the World Polity." *American Journal of Sociology* 115, no. 4: 1018–1068. https://doi.org/10.1086/649577.

Beckwith, Karen. 2001. "Gender Frames and Collective Action: Configurations of Masculinity in the Pittston Coal Strike." *Politics & Society* 29, no. 2 (June): 297–330. https://doi.org/10.1177/0032329201029002006.

Beer, Michael. 2021. *Civil Resistance Tactics in the 21st Century.* Washington, DC: International Center on Nonviolent Conflict.

Beissinger, Mark R. 2002. *Nationalist Mobilization and the Collapse of the Soviet State.* Cambridge: Cambridge University Press.

Benavot, Aaron, and Phyllis Riddle. 1988. "The Expansion of Primary Education 1870–1940: Trends and Issues." *Sociology of Education* 61 (July): 190–210.

Berkovitch, Nitza. 1999. *From Motherhood to Citizenship: Women's Rights and International Organizations.* Baltimore, MD: Johns Hopkins University Press.

Berkovitch, Nitza, and Karen Bradley. 1999. "The Globalization of Women's Status: Consensus/Dissensus in the World Polity." *Sociological Perspectives* 42, no. 3 (September): 481–498. https://doi.org/10.2307/1389699.

Berman, Eli, and David A. Lake. 2019. *Proxy Wars: Suppressing Violence through Local Agents.* Ithaca, NY: Cornell University Press.

Blumberg, Herbert H., A. Paul Hare, and Anna Costin. 2006. *Peace Psychology: A Comprehensive Introduction.* New York: Cambridge University Press.

Boff, Leonardo. 1991. "Active Nonviolence: The Political and Moral Power of the Poor." In *Relentless Persistence: Nonviolent Action in Latin America*, edited by Philip McManus and Gerald Schlabach, vii–xi. Gabriola Island, BC: New Society.

Boli, John. 1987. *World-Polity Sources of Expanding State Authority and Organization, 1870–1970.* Newbury Park: SAGE.

Boli, John. 2006. "The Rationalization of Virtue and Virtuosity in World Society." In *Transnational Governance: Institutional Dynamics of Regulation*, edited by Marie-Laure Djelic and Kerstin Sahlin-Andersson, 95–118. Cambridge: Cambridge University Press.

Boli, John, and Frank J. Lechner. 2005. *World Culture: Origins and Consequences.* Malden, MA: Wiley-Blackwell.

Boli, John, and George M. Thomas. 1997. "World Culture in the World Polity: A Century of International Non-Governmental Organization." *American Sociological Review* 62, no. 2 (April): 171–190. https://doi.org/10.2307/2657298.

Boli, John, and George M. Thomas. 1999. *Constructing World Culture: International Nongovernmental Organizations since 1875*. Palo Alto, CA: Stanford University Press.

Boli, John, Selina Gallo-Cruz, and Matt Mathias. 2011. "World Polity Theory." In *The International Studies Compendium Project*, edited by Robert A. Denemark. Oxford: Blackwell.

Boston Daily Globe. 1922. "The Threat of Non-Violence." *ProQuest Historical Newspapers*.

Boulding, Elise. 2000. *Cultures of Peace: The Hidden Side of History*. Syracuse, NY: Syracuse University Press.

Boyle, Elizabeth Heger. 2006. *Female Genital Cutting: Cultural Conflict in the Global Community*. Baltimore, MD: Johns Hopkins University Press.

Brecke, Peter. 1999. "Violent Conflicts 1400 A.D. to the Present in Different Regions of the World." Paper Prepared for the 1999 Meeting of the Peace Science Society (International), Ann Arbor, MI, October 8–10, 1999.

Bromley, Patricia, Evan Schofer, and Wesley Longhofer. 2018. "Organizing for Education: A Cross-National, Longitudinal Study of Civil Society Organizations and Education Outcomes." *Voluntas: International Journal of Nonprofit and Voluntary Organizations* 29: 526–540.

Brulle, Robert J., and Carter Werthman. 2021. "The Role of Public Relations Firms in Climate Change Politics." *Climatic Change* 169, no. (1–2): 8. https://doi.org/10.1007/s10584-021-03244-4.

Bruyn, Severyn T., and Paula Rayman. 1979. *Nonviolent Action and Social Change*. New York: John Wiley.

Bryant, Lisa. 2011. "Sarkozy: Critical That G8 Support Arab 'Spring'." *VOA*. www.voanews.com/a/sarkozy-critical-that-g8-support-arab-spring-122687034/139951.html. Accessed November 6, 2023.

Casanova, José. 1994. *Public Religions in the Modern World*. Chicago, IL: The University of Chicago Press.

Case, Benjamin. 2021. "Molotov Cocktails to Mass Marches: Strategic Nonviolence, Symbolic Violence, and the Mobilizing Effect of Riots." *Theory in Action* 14, no. 1: 18–38.

Case, Clarence. 1923. *Non-violent Coercion: A Study in the Methods of Social Pressure*. New York: Garland.

Cebul, Matthew D., and Jonathan Pinckney. 2022. "Nonviolent Action in the Era of Digital Authoritarianism." *United States Institute of Peace Special Report*. www.usip.org/publications/2022/02/nonviolent-action-era-digital-authoritarianism-hardships-and-innovations. Accessed July 6, 2023.

Chabot, Sean. 2000. "Transnational Diffusion and the African American Reinvention of Gandhian Repertoire." *Mobilization: An International Quarterly* 5, no. 2: 201–216.

Chabot, Sean. 2011. *Transnational Roots of the Civil Rights Movement: African American Explorations of the Gandhian Repertoire.* Lanham, MD: Lexington Books.

Chabot, Sean, and Majid Sharifi. 2013. "The Violence of Nonviolence: Problematizing Nonviolent Resistance in Iran and Egypt." *Societies without Borders* 8, no. 2: 205–232. https://scholarlycommons.law.case.edu/swb/vol8/iss2/2.

Chamberlain, Muriel Evelyn. 1999. *Decolonization: The Fall of European Empires.* London: Wiley-Blackwell.

Chase-Dunn, Christopher. 1999. "Globalization: A World-Systems Perspective." *Journal of World-Systems Research* 5, no. 2: 186–215. https://doi.org/10.5195/jwsr.1999.134.

Chatfield, Charles, ed. 1973. *Peace Movements in America.* New York: Schocken Books.

Chenoweth, Erica. 2019. "NAVCO Data Project Version History and Description Guide." *Harvard Dataverse.* https://doi.org/10.7910/DVN/CQFXXM.

Chenoweth, Erica. 2021. Keynote Address: *Between Peril and Potential.* Dayton, OH: University of Dayton School of Law.

Chenoweth, Erica. 2022. "Can Nonviolent Resistance Survive COVID-19?" *Journal of Human Rights* 21, no. 3: 304–316.

Chenoweth, Erica, and Maria J. Stephan. 2011. *Why Civil Resistance Works: The Strategic Logic of Nonviolent Conflict.* New York: Columbia University Press.

Chenoweth, Erica, and Maria J. Stephan. 2021. "The Role of External Support in Nonviolent Campaigns: Poisoned Chalice or Holy Grail?" Washington, DC: International Center on Nonviolent Conflict. www.nonviolent-conflict.org/external-support-for-nonviolent-campaigns.

Chenoweth, Erica, and Orion A. Lewis. 2013. "Unpacking Nonviolent Campaigns: Introducing the NAVCO 2.0 Dataset." *Journal of Peace Research* 50, no. 3: 415–423. https://doi.org/10.1177/0022343312471551.

Chenoweth, Erica, Jonathan Pinckney, and Orion A. Lewis. 2019. "NAVCO 3.0 Dataset." *Harvard Dataverse.* https://doi.org/10.7910/DVN/INNYEO.

Choi, Hyaeweol. 1999. "The Societal Impact of Student Politics in Contemporary South Korea." *Higher Education* 22: 175–188. https://doi.org/10.1007/BF00137475.

Christoyannopoulos, Alexandre. 2022. "An Anarcho-Pacifist Reading of International Relations: A Normative Critique of International Politics from the Confluence of Pacifism and Anarchism." *International Studies Quarterly* 66, no. 4 (December): sqac070. https://doi.org/10.1093/isq/sqac070.

Chua, Lynette. 2018. *The Politics of Love in Myanmar: LGBT Mobilization and Human Rights as a Way of Life*. Palo Alto, CA: Stanford University Press.

Clark, Rob. 2010. "Technical and Institutional States: Loose Coupling in the Human Rights Sector of the World Polity." *The Sociological Quarterly* 51, no. 1: 65–95, https://doi.org/10.1111/j.1533-8525.2009.01163.x.

Cole, Wade M. 2017. "World Polity or World Society? Delineating the Statist and Societal Dimensions of the Global Institutional System." *International Sociology* 32, no. 1: 86–104. https://doi.org/10.1177/0268580916675526.

Cole, Wade M. 2020. "Working to Protect Rights: Women's Civil Liberties in Cross-Cultural Perspective." *Social Science Research* 91 (September). https://doi.org/10.1016/j.ssresearch.2020.102461.

Cole, Wade M., and Gaëlle Perrier. 2019. "Political Equality for Women and the Poor: Assessing the Effects and Limits of World Society, 1975–2010." *International Journal of Comparative Sociology* 60, no. 3: 140–172. https://doi.org/10.1177/0020715219831422.

Cornell, Andrew. 2011. *Oppose and Propose: Lessons from Movement for a New Society*. Oakland, CA: AK Press.

Cortright, David. 2008. *Peace: A History of Movements and Ideas*. Cambridge: Cambridge University Press.

Dandeker, Christopher, ed. 1998. *Nationalism and Violence*. New Bruinswick, NJ: Transaction.

Danielson, Leilah. 2014. *American Gandhi: A. J. Muste and the History of Radicalism in the Twentieth Century*. Politics and Culture in Modern America. Philadelphia, PA: University of Pennsylvania Press.

Darboe, Alieu. 2010. "Senegal: 1974-Present." *International Center on Nonviolent Conflict*. www.nonviolent-conflict.org/senegal-1974-present. Accessed November 6, 2023.

Davies, Thomas Richard Davies. 2014. "The Failure of Strategic Nonviolent Action in Bahrain, Egypt, Libya and Syria: 'Political ju-jitsu' in Reverse." *Global Change, Peace & Security* 26, no. 3: 299–313. https://doi.org/10.1080/14781158.2014.924916.

de la Torre, Carlos, and Enrique Peruzzotti. 2018. "Populism in Power: Between Inclusion and Autocracy." *Populism* 1: 38–58. https://doi.org/10.1163/25888072-01011002.

Devetak, Richard, and Christopher W. Hughes. 2008. *The Globalization of Political Violence: Globalization's Shadow*. New York: Taylor and Francis.

Diwakar, Ranganath Ramachandra, and Gandhi Smarak Nidhi. 1964. *Gandhi: His Relevance for Our Times*. Berkeley, CA: World without War Council.

Doward, Jamie. 2011. "UK Training Saudi Forces Used to Crush Arab Spring." *The Guardian*, May 28, www.theguardian.com/world/2011/may/28/uk-training-saudi-troops.

Downey, Gary L. 1986. "Ideology and the Clamshell Identity: Organizational Dilemmas in the Anti-Nuclear Power Movement." *Social Problems* 33, no. 5: 357–373. https://doi.org/10.2307/800656.

Drori, Gili S. 2008. "Institutionalism and Globalization Studies." In *Handbook of Organizational Institutionalism*, edited by Royston Greenwood, Christine Oliver, Kerstin Sahlin-Andersson, and Roy Suddaby, 798–842. Thousand Oaks, CA: SAGE.

Drori, Gili S., John W. Meyer, and Hokyu Hwang. 2006. *Globalization and Organization: World Society and Organizational Change*. Oxford: Oxford University Press.

Duvall, Jack. 2004. "Power by the People." *Vital Speeches of the Day* 71, no. 1: 2–9.

Easwaran, Eknath. 1999. *Nonviolent Soldier of Islam: Badshah Khan, a Man to Match His Mountains*. Tomales, CA: Nilgiri Press.

Echols, Alice. 1992. "The Taming of the Id: Feminist Sexual Politics." In *Pleasure and Danger*, edited by Carol Vance, 50–72. London: Routledge.

Echols, Alice. 2019. *Daring to Be Bad: Radical Feminism in America 1967–1975, Thirtieth Anniversary Edition*. Minneapolis, MN: University of Minnesota Press.

Edgarton, David. 2007. *The Shock of the Old: Technology and Global History since 1900*. Oxford: Oxford University Press.

Elliott, Michael. 2009. "A Cult of the Individual for a Global Society: The Development and Worldwide Expansion of Human Rights Ideology." PhD diss. Emory University.

Engler, Mark. 2013. "The Machiavelli of Nonviolence: Gene Sharp and the Battle against Corporate Rule." *Dissent Magazine*. www.dissentmagazine.org/article/the-machiavelli-of-nonviolence-gene-sharp-and-the-battle-against-corporate-rule. Accessed November 6, 2023.

Engle, Eric. 2014. "A New Cold War? Cold Peace. Russia, Ukraine, and NATO." *Saint Louis University Law Journal* 59, no. 1 (Fall): 97–173. https://scholarship.law.slu.edu/lj/vol59/iss1/5.

Ennis, James G. 1987. "Fields of Action: Structure in Tactical Repertoires." *Sociological Forum* 2, no. 3 (Summer 1987): 520–533. https://link.springer.com/article/10.1007/BF01106624.

Eschle, Catherine, and Neil Stammers. 2004. "Taking Part: Social Movements, INGOs, and Global Change." *Alternatives* 29, no. 3: 333–372. https://doi.org/10.1177/030437540402900305.

Eyre, Dana P., and Mark C. Suchman. 1996. "Status, Norms and the Proliferation of Conventional Weapons: An Institutional Theory Approach." In *The Culture of National Security: Norms and Identity in World Politics*, edited by Peter J. Katzenstein, 79-113. New York: Columbia University Press.

Ferree, Myra Marx, and David A. Merrill. 2000. "Hot Movements, Cold Cognition: Thinking about Social Movements in Gendered Frames." *Contemporary Sociology* 29, no. 3 (May): 454–462. https://doi.org/ 10.2307/2653932.

Fisher, Frederick Bohn. 1932. *That Strange Little Brown Man Gandhi*. New York: R. Long & R. R. Smith.

Florini, Ann, ed. 2000. *The Third Force: The Rise of Transnational Civil Society*. Washington DC: Carnegie Endowment for International Peace.

Frank, David John, and Elizabeth H. McEneaney. 1999. "The Individualization of Society and the Liberalization of State Policies on Same-Sex Sexual Relations, 1984–1995." *Social Forces* 77, no. 3 (March): 911–943. https:// doi.org/10.2307/3005966.

Frank, David John, and John W. Meyer. 2002. "The Profusion of Individual Roles and Identities in the Postwar Period." *Sociological Theory* 20, no. 1 (March): 86–105. www.jstor.org/stable/3108657.

Frank, David John, Wesley Longhofer, and Evan Schofer. 2007. "World Society, NGOs, and Environmental Policy Reform in Asia." *International Journal of Comparative Sociology* 48, no. 4: 275–295. https://doi.org/ 10.1177/0020715207079530.

Fridman, Orli. 2011. "'It Was Like Fighting a War with Our Own People': Anti-War Activism in Serbia during the 1990s." *Nationalities Papers* 39, no. 4: 507–522. https://doi.org/10.1080/00905992.2011.579953.

Friends Service Council. 1947. "History of the Organization." *The Nobel Peace Prize Friends Service Council.* www.nobelprize.org/prizes/peace/1947/ friends-committee/history/. Accessed July 6, 2023.

Gaines, Kevin K. 2007. *African Americans in Ghana: Black Expatriates and the Civil Rights Era*. Chapel Hill, NC: University of North Carolina Press.

Gallo-Cruz, Selina. 2012. "Organizing Global Nonviolence: The Growth and Spread of Nonviolent INGOS, 1948–2003." In *Nonviolent Conflict and Civil Resistance*, Research in Social Movements, Conflicts and Change, Vol. 34, edited by Sharon Erickson Nepstad and Lester R. Kurtz, 213–256. Bingley: Emerald Group.

Gallo-Cruz, Selina. 2015. "Protest and Public Relations: The Reinvention of the US Army School of the Americas" *Interface*: *A Journal for and about Social Movements* 7, no. 1: 322–350.

Gallo-Cruz, Selina. 2016a. "More Powerful Forces? Women, Nonviolence, and Mobilization." *Sociology Compass* 10, no. 9 (September): 823–835. https://doi.org/10.1111/soc4.12405.

Gallo-Cruz, Selina. 2016b. "Weaving Political Fields: Non-violent INGOs and the Global Grass Roots." *European Journal of Cultural and Political Sociology* 3, no. (2–3): 243–279. https://doi.org/10.1080/23254823.2016.1210526.

Gallo-Cruz, Selina. 2016c. "The Insufficient Imagery of Top-Down, Bottom-Up in Global Movements Analysis." *Social Movement Studies* 16, no. 2: 153–168. https://doi.org/10.1080/14742837.2016.1252664.

Gallo-Cruz, Selina. 2019. "Nonviolence beyond the State: International NGOs and Local Nonviolent Mobilization." *International Sociology* 34, no. 6: 655–674. https://doi.org/10.1177/0268580919865100.

Gallo-Cruz, Selina. 2021a. "Marginalization and Mobilizing Power in Nonviolent Social Movements." In *Power and Protest*, Research in *Social Movements, Conflicts and Change*, Vol. 44, edited by Lisa Leitz, 91–115. Bingley: Emerald.

Gallo-Cruz, Selina. 2021b. *Political Invisibility and Mobilization: Women against State Violence in Argentina, Yugoslavia, and Liberia*. London: Routledge.

Galtung, Johan. 1956. "Institutionalized Conflict Resolution: A Theoretical Paradigm." *Journal of Peace Research* 2, no. 4: 348–397. https://doi.org/10.1177/002234336500200404.

Galtung, Johan. 1969. "Violence, Peace, and Peace Research." *Journal of Peace Research* 6, no. 3: 167–191.

Galtung, Johan. 1990. "Cultural Violence." *Journal of Peace Research* 27, no. 3: 291–305. https://doi.org/10.1177/0022343390027003005.

Galtung, Johan. 2011a. "Arne Næss, Peace and Gandhi." *Inquiry* 54, no. 1: 31–41, https://doi.org//10.1080/0020174X.2011.542948.

Galtung, Johan. 2011b. "Peace, Positive and Negative." *The Encyclopedia of Peace Psychology*. https://doi.org/10.1002/9780470672532.wbepp189.

Galtung, Johan, and Dietrich Fisher. 2013. *Johan Galtung: Pioneer of Peace Research*. Berlin: Springer.

Gamson, William A. 1975. *The Strategy of Social Protest*. Homewood, IL: Dorsey Press.

Gandhi, Mohandas K. 1946. "A Message for the I.N.A." In *My Non-violence*, edited by Sailesh Kumar Bandopadhyaya. Ahemadabad: Navajivan Trust. www.mkgandhi.org/mynonviolence/chap77.

Ganguly, Debjani, and John Docker. 2008. *Rethinking Gandhi and Nonviolent Relationality*. New York: Routledge.

Garraty, John A., and Peter Gay. 1972. *The Columbia History of the World*. New York: Harper & Row.

Gelderloos, Peter. 2013. *The Failure of Nonviolence: From the Arab Spring to Occupy*. St. Louis, MO: Left Bank Books.

Gelderloos, Peter. 2020. "Debunking the Myths around Nonviolent Resistance." *ROAR*, August 22, 2020. https://roarmag.org/essays/chenoweth-stephan-nonvi olence-myth.

Giugni, Marco. 2009. "Political Opportunities: From Tilly to Tilly." *Swiss Political Science Review* 15, no. 2: 361–368.

Giugni, Marco, and Maria Grasso. 2015. "Environmental Movements, Heterogeneity, Transformation, and Institutionalization." *Annual Review of Environment and Resources* 40: 337–361.

Goldstone, Jack A. 2003. *States, Parties, and Social Movements*. New York: Cambridge University Press.

Gómez-Upegui, Salomé. 2021. "The Amazon Rainforest's Most Dogged Defenders Are in Peril." *Vox*, September 1, 2021. www.vox.com/down-to-earth/22641038/indigenous-forest-guardians-brazil-guajajara.

Gregg, Richard. 1935. *The Power of Non-Violence*. Philadelphia, PA: J. B. Lippincott.

Guriev, Sergei, and Daniel Treisman. 2022. *Spin Dictators: The Changing Face of Tyranny in the 21st Century*. Princeton, TX: Princeton University Press.

Gurr, Ted R., Monty G. Marshall, and Keith Jaggers. 2010. "Polity IV Project: Political Regime Characteristics and Transitions, 1800–2010." *The Center for Systemic Peace*. www.systemicpeace.org/polityproject.html. Accessed July 6, 2023.

Hanbury, Shanna. 2019. "Murders of Indigenous Leaders in Brazilian Amazon Hits Highest Level in Two Decades." *Mongabay*, December 14, 2019. https://news.mongabay.com/2019/12/murders-of-indigenous-leaders-in-brazil-amazon-hit-highest-level-in-two-decades.

Hare, A. Paul, and Herbert Blumberg. 1968. *Non-violent Direct Action. American Cases: Social Psychological Analyses*. Washington, DC: Corpus Books.

Hare, A. Paul, and Herbert Blumberg. 1977. *Liberation without Violence*. Totowa, NJ: Rowman and Littlefield.

Held, David, Anthony McGrew, David Goldblatt, and Jonathan Perraton. 1999. *Global Transformations: Politics, Economics, and Culture*. Stanford, CA: Stanford University Press.

Hemment, Julie. 2007. *Empowering Women in Russia: Activism, Aid, and NGOs*. Bloomington, IN: Indiana University Press.

Hironaka, Ann. 2008. *Neverending Wars the International Community, Weak States, and the Perpetuation of Civil War*. Cambridge, MA: Harvard University Press.

Hironaka, Ann. 2014. *Greening the Globe*. New York: Cambridge University Press.

Holton, Paul, and Mark Bromley. 2010. "The International Arms Trade: Difficult to Define, Measure, and Control." *Arms Control Today* 40, no. 6 (July/August): 8–14. www.armscontrol.org/act/2010-07/international-arms-trade-difficult-define-measure-control.

Hope, Marjorie, and James Young. 1977. *The Struggle for Humanity: Agents of Nonviolent Change in a Violent World*. Maryknoll, NY: Orbis Books.

Hunter, Robert. 2022. "The Ukraine Crisis: Why and What Now?" *Survival: Global Politics and Strategy* 64, no. 1: 7–28. https://doi.org/10.1080/00396338.2022.2032953.

Innes, Michael A. 2012. *Making Sense of Proxy Wars: States, Surrogates & the Use of Force*. Washington, DC: Potomac Books.

International Center on Nonviolent Conflict. 2016. "Frequently Asked Questions." www.nonviolent-conflict.org/frequently-asked-questions.

Jang, Yong Suk. 2003. "The Global Diffusion of Ministries of Science and Technology." In *Science in the Modern World Polity: Institutionalization and Globalization*, edited by Gili S. Drori, John W. Meyer, Francisco O. Ramirez, and Evan Schofer, 120–135. Stanford, CA: Stanford University Press.

Janoski, Thomas, Robert Alford, Alexander Hicks, and Mildred A. Schwartz, eds. 2005. *Handbook of Political Sociology: States, Civil Societies, and Globalization*. New York: Cambridge University Press.

Jepperson, Ronald L. 1991. "Institutions, Institutional Effects, and Institution-alism." In *The New Institutionalism in Organizational Analysis*, edited by Walter W. Powell and Paul DiMaggio, 143–163. Chicago: University of Chicago Press.

Juppé, Alain. 2011. "Arab Spring: Hopes and Challenges." Transcript of Speech Delivered at the Arab World Institute, Paris, April 15, 2011. https://www.brookings.edu/events/the-arab-spring-hopes-and-challenges/

Jupille, Joseph, Brandy Jolliff, and Stefan Wojcik. 2013. *Regionalism in the World Polity*. March 28. https://ssrn.com/abstract=2242500.

Kadivar, Mohammed Ali. 2022. *Popular Politics and the Path to Durable Democracy*. Princeton, TX: Princeton University Press.

Kalb, Martin. 2015. *Imperial Gamble: Putin, Ukraine and the New Cold War*. Washington, DC: Brookings Institution Press.

King, Martin Luther, Jr. 1958. *Stride toward Freedom*. New York: Harper.

Kling, Blair B. 1991. "Gandhi, Nonviolence, and the Holocaust." *Peace & Change: A Journal of Peace Research* 16, no. 2: 176–196.

Koenig, Mattias. 2008. "Institutional Change in the World Polity: International Human Rights and the Construction of Collective Identities." *International Sociology* 23, no. 1: 95–114. https://doi.org/10.1177/0268580907084387.

Krücken, Georg, and Gili Drori. 2009. *World Society: The Writings of John W. Meyer.* Oxford: Oxford University Press.

Kubik, Jan. 1998. "Institutionalization of Protest during Democratic Consolidations in Central Europe." In *The Social Movement Society: Contentious Politics for a New Century,* edited by David S. Meyer and Sidney Tarrow, 131–152. Lanham, MD: Rowman and Littlefield.

Kuppuswamy, C. S. 2011. "Sino-Myanmar Relations and Its Impact on the Region." *Eurasia Review,* March 3. www.eurasiareview.com/03032011-sino-myanmar-relations-and-its-impact-on-the-region.

Kurzman, Charles. 2004. "Can Understanding Undermine Explanation? The Confused Experience of Revolution." *Philosophy of the Social Sciences* 34, no. 3 (September): 328–351. https://doi.org/10.1177/0048393104266687.

LaFree, Gary, Min Xie, and Aila M. Matanock . 2018. "Contagious Diffusion of World-Wide Terrorism: It Is Less Common Than We Might Think." *Studies in Conflict and Terrorism* 41, no. 4: 261–280.

Lakey, George. 1968. *The Sociological Mechanisms of Non-Violent Action.* Oakville: Peace Research Institute.

Lakey, George. 1987. *Powerful Peacemaking: A Strategy for a Living Revolution.* Philadelphia, PA: New Society.

Lakey, George. 2019. "Will the Real Gene Sharp Please Step Forward?" *Waging Nonviolence: People-Powered News and Analysis.* July 16. https://wagingnonviolence.org/2019/07/gene-sharp-cold-war-intellectual-marcie-smith/. Accessed July 6, 2023.

Lambelet, Kyle BT. 2021. "Nonviolent Struggle between Norm and Technique." *Journal of International Political Theory* 18, no. 2: 148–166. https://doi.org/10.1177/17550882211039747.

Lawson, George. 2019. *Anatomies of Revolutions.* Cambridge: Cambridge University Press.

Lechner, Frank J. 2009. *Globalization: The Making of World Society.* Chinchester: Wiley-Blackwell.

Lechner, Frank, and John Boli. 2005. *World Culture: Origins and Consequences.* Malden, MA: Blackwell.

Lehoucq, Fabrice. 2016. "Review: Does Nonviolence Work?" *Comparative Politics* 48, no. 2: 269–287. https://doi.org/10.5129/001041516817037691.

Levitt, Peggy, and Sally Merry. 2009. "Vernacularization on the Ground: Local Uses of Global Women's Rights in Peru, China, India and the United States." *Global Networks* 9, no. 4 (October): 441–461. https://doi.org/10.1111/j.1471-0374.2009.00263.x.

Long, Michael G. 2021. *We the Resistance: Documenting a History of Nonviolent Protest in the United States.* San Francisco, CA: City Lights Books.

Longhofer, Wesley, Evan Schofer, Natasha Miric, and David John Frank. 2016. "NGOs, INGOs, and Environmental Policy Reform, 1970–2010." *Social Forces* 94, no. 4 (June): 1743–1768.

Los Angeles Times. 1921. "Free Burma: The Demand." *ProQuest Historical Newspapers.*

Louise, Christopher. 1995. "The Social Impacts of Light Weapons Availability and Proliferation." Geneva: United Nations Research Institute for Social Development.

Macleod, Jason. 2015. *Merdeka and the Morning Star: Civil Resistance in West Papua.* Saint Lucia: University of Queensland Press.

Mandić, Danilo. 2021. *Gangsters and Other Statesmen: Mafias, Separatists, and Torn States in a Globalized World.* Princeton, TX: Princeton University Press.

Mann, Michael. 1994. "In Praise of Macro-Sociology: A Reply to Goldthorpe." *The British Journal of Sociology* 45, no. 1 (March): 37–54. https://doi.org/10.2307/591524.

Manohka, Ivan. 2009. "Foucault's Concept of Power and the Global Discourse of Human Rights." *Global Society* 23, no. 4: 429–452. https://doi.org/10.1080/13600820903198792.

Markoff, John. 1996. *Waves of Democracy: Social Movements and Political Change.* Thousand Oaks, CA: Pine Forge Press.

Mason, Christine. 2005. "Women, Violence and Nonviolent Resistance in East Timor." *Journal of Peace Research* 42, no. 6 (November): 737–749. https://doi.org/10.1177/0022343305057890.

Masuhara, Takaaki, Toru Kuriyama, Masakazu Yoshida, and Jun Cheng. 2015. "Formal Verification of Robertson-Type Uncertainty Relation." *Journal of Quantum Information Science* 5, no. 2 (June): 58–70. https://doi.org/10.4236/jqis.2015.52008.

McAllister, Pam. 1982. *Reweaving the Web of Life: Feminism and Nonviolence.* Philadelphia, PA: New Society.

McCammon, Holly J. 2003. "Out of the Parlors and into the Streets: The Changing Tactical Repertoire of the U.S. Women's Suffrage Movements." *Social Forces* 81, no. 3 (March): 787–818. https://doi.org/10.1353/sof.2003.0037.

McCammon, Holly J., and Lee Ann Banaszak, eds. 2018. *100 Years of the Nineteenth Amendment: An Appraisal of Women's Political Activism.* New York: Oxford University Press.

McCarthy, Eli S. 2021. "What a Truly Humanitarian Response in Afghanistan Would Look Like." Analysis. *Waging Nonviolence*, August 24. https://wagingnonviolence.org/2021/08/what-a-truly-humanitarian-response-in-afghanistan-would-look-like/.

McCarthy, John D., and Clark McPhail. 1998. "Policing Protest in France and Italy: From Intimidation to Cooperation?" In *The Social Movement Society Contentious Politics for a New Century*, edited by David Meyer and Sydney Tarrow. Lanham: Rowman & Littlefield.

McCully, Murray. 2011. "Murray McCully Speech: The Arab Spring." *Scoop Independent News*, August 2. www.scoop.co.nz/stories/PA1108/S00015/murray-mccully-speech-the-arab-spring.htm.

McGuinness, Kate. 1993. "Gene Sharp's Theory of Power: A Feminist Critique of Consent." *Journal of Peace Research* 30, no. 1 (February): 101–115. https://doi.org/10.1177/0022343393030001011.

McManus, Philip, and Gerald Schlabach. 1991. *Relentless Persistence: Nonviolent Action in Latin America*. Philadelphia, PA: New Society.

Merry, Sally Engle. 2006. *Human Rights and Gender Violence Translating International Law into Local Justice*. Chicago, IL: The University of Chicago Press.

Merry, Sally Engle, and Peggy Levitt. 2017. "The Vernacularization of Women's Human Rights." In *Human Rights Futures*, edited by Stephen Hopgood, Jack Snyder, and Leslie Vinjamuri, 213–236. Cambridge: Cambridge University Press.

Meyer, David S. 1990. *A Winter of Discontent: The Nuclear Freeze and American Politics*. New York: Praeger.

Meyer, David S. 2019. "How the Effectiveness of Nonviolent Action is the Wrong Question for Activists, Academics, and Everyone Else" In *Nonviolent Resistance and the State*, edited by Hank Johnston, 151–161. Abindon: Routledge

Meyer, David S., and Nancy Whittier. 1994. "Social Movement Spillover." *Social Problems* 41, no. 2 (May): 277–298. https://doi.org/10.2307/3096934.

Meyer, David S., and Sidney G. Tarrow. 1998. *The Social Movement Society: Contentious Politics for a New Century*. Lanham, MD: Rowman & Littlefield.

Meyer, John W., John Boli, George M. Thomas, and Francisco O. Ramirez. 1997. "World Society and the Nation-State." *American Journal of Sociology* 103, no. 1 (July): 144–181. https://doi.org/10.1086/231174.

Meyer, John W., and Ron L. Jepperson. 2000. "The "Actors" of Modern Society: The Cultural Construction of Social Agency." *Sociological Theory* 18, no. 1: 100–120. https://doi.org/10.1111/0735-2751.00090.

Mietzner, Marcus. 2020a. "Rival Populisms and the Democratic Crisis in Indonesia: Chauvinists, Islamists and Technocrats." *Australian Journal of International Affairs* 74, no. 4: 420–438.

Mietzner, Marcus. 2020b. "Authoritarian Innovations in Indonesia: Electoral Narrowing, Identity Politics and Executive Illiberalism." *Democratization*, 27, no. 6: 1021–1036. https://doi.org/10.1080/13510347.2019.1704266.

Morris, Aldon. 1984. *The Origins of the Civil Rights Movement: Black Communities Organizing for Change*. New York: The Free Press.

Morton, Joe. 1998. "Fundamental Relations between Nonviolence and Human Rights." *Journal of the Gandhi-King Society* 9, no. 2 (Fall): 19–31. https://doi.org/10.5840/acorn1998923.

Moser-Puangsuwan, Yeshua, and Thomas Weber. 2000. *Nonviolent Intervention across Borders*. Honolulu: Spark M. Matsunaga Institute for Peace, University of Hawai'i.

Mueller, Carol. 1999. "Escape from the GDR, 1961–1989: Hybrid Exit Repertoires in a Disintegrating Leninist Regime." *American Journal of Sociology* 105, no. 3 (November): 697–735. https://doi.org/10.1086/210358.

Navarro, J. G. 2023. "PR Industry Market Size Worldwide, 2022–2027." *Statista*. www.statista.com/statistics/645836/public-relations-pr-revenue/. Accessed July 6, 2023.

Nepstad, Sharon. 2011. *Nonviolent Revolutions: Civil Resistance in the Late 20th Century*. Oxford: Oxford University Press.

Nesbitt, Katherine, and Stephen Zunes. 2009. "Mali's March Revolution (1991)." *International Center on Nonviolent Conflict*. Accessed December 9, 2022. www.nonviolent-conflict.org/malis-march-revolution-1991/.

Offen, Karen. n.d. *Gandhi, the English Suffragists and Nonviolent Direct Action*. San Francisco, CA: International Museum of Women.

Ojeme, Victoria. 2021. "PCR Calls for Non-Violent Approach to Conflict Resolution." *Vanguardngr*, September 17. www.vanguardngr.com/2021/09/ipcr-calls-for-non-violent-approach-to-conflict-resolution/.

Olzak, Susan. 1989. "Analysis of Events in the Study of Collective Action." *Annual Review of Sociology* 15: 119–141.

Oo, Zarchi, Billy Ford, and Jonathan Pinckney. 2021 "Myanmar in the Streets: A Nonviolent Movement Shows Staying Power." *US Institute of Peace*, March 31. www.usip.org/publications/2021/03/myanmar-streets-nonviolent-movement-shows-staying-power.

Oreskes, Naomi, and Erik M. Conway. 2010. *Merchants of Doubt: How a Handful of Scientists Obscured the Truth on Issues from Tobacco Smoke to Global Warming*. New York: Bloomsbury.

Paxton, Robin. 2011. "INTERVIEW-Kazakh PM Says Opposition Needed in Parliament." *Reuters*, April 2. https://jp.reuters.com/article/kazakhstan-election-pm-idAFLDE73100D20110402.

Peace Brigades International 1981. Founding Statement.

Peck, Tom. 2011. "Arab Spring Refugees Not Welcome Here, Says William Hague." *Independent*, May 23. www.independent.co.uk/news/uk/politics/arab-spring-refugees-not-welcome-here-says-william-hague-2287795.

Pinckney, Jonathan. 2020. *From Dissent to Democracy: The Promise and Peril of Civil Resistance Transitions*. Oxford: Oxford University Press.

Polo, Sara M. T. 2020. "How Terrorism Spreads: Emulation and the Diffusion of Ethnic and Ethnoreligious Terrorism." *Journal of Conflict Resolution* 64, no. 10 (November): 1916–1942. https://doi.org/10.1177/0022002720930811.

Poonawalla, Aziz. 2011. "Transcript and Word Cloud of Obama's 'Moment of Opportunity'. " *Beliefnet*. www.beliefnet.com/columnists/cityofbrass/2011/05/transcript-and-word-cloud-of-obamas-moment-of-opportunity-mespeech.html.

Pruijt, Hans, and Conny Roggeband. 2014. "Autonomous and/or Institutionalized Social Movements? Conceptual Clarification and Illustrative Cases." *International Journal of Comparative Sociology* 55, no. 2 (April): 144–165. https://doi.org/10.1177/0020715214537847.

Ramachandran, G. and T. K. Mahadevan, eds. 1967. *Gandhi: His Relevance for Our Times*. Berkeley, CA: World without War Council.

Ramirez, Francisco O., and Elizabeth H. McEneaney. 1997. "From Women's Suffrage to Reproduction Rights? Cross-National Considerations." *International Journal of Comparative Sociology* 38: 24–26. https://doi.org/10.1177/002071529703800102.

Randle, Michael. 1994. *Civil Resistance*. London: Fontana Press.

Ray, Raka. 1999. *Fields of Protest: Women's Movements in India*. Minneapolis, MN: University of Minnesota Press.

Reilly, James. 2013. "China and Japan in Myanmar: Aid, Natural Resources and Influence." *Asian Studies Review* 37, no. 2: 141–157. https://doi.org/10.1080/10357823.2013.767310.

Reuschemeyer, Dietrich, and John D. Stephens. 1997. "Comparing Historical Sequences: A Powerful Tool for Causal Analysis." *Comparative Social Research* 16: 55–72.

Rist, Gilbert. 2019. *The History of Development: From Western Origins to Global Faith*. London: Zed Books.

Ritter, Daniel. 2015. *The Iron Cage of Liberalism: International Politics and Unarmed Revolutions in the Middle East and North Africa*. Oxford: Oxford University Press.

Robertson, Roland. 1992. *Globalization: Social Theory and Global Culture*. London: SAGE.

Roy, Olivier. 2004. *Globalized Islam: The Search for a New Ummah*. New York: Columbia University Press.

Rucht, Dieter, and Friedhelm Neidhardt. 2002. "Towards a 'Movement Society'? On the Possibilities of Institutionalizing Social Movements." *Social Movement Studies* 1, no. 1: 7–30.

Rudd, Kevin. 2011. "Keep the Faith with the Arab Spring." *The Australian*, 8.

Rupesinghe, Kumar, Marcial C. Rubio, and UN University. 1994. *The Culture of Violence*. Tokyo, New York, Paris: United Nations University Press. https://digitallibrary.un.org/record/198767.

Salla, Michael. 1995. "East Timor's Nonviolent Resistance." *Peace Review* 7, no. 2: 191–197. https://doi.org/10.1080/10402659508425875.

Salla, Michael. 1995. "Kosovo, Non-Violence and the Break-Up of Yugoslavia." *Security Dialogue* 26, no. 4 (December): 427–438. https://doi.org/10.1177/0967010695026004008.

Sarkees, Meredith Reid, and Phil Schafer. 2000. "The Correlates of War Data on War: An Update to 1997." *Conflict Management and Peace Science* 18, no. 1 (February): 123–144. https://doi.org/10.1177/073889420001800105.

Sasaran, Eli. 2006. "A Consistent Ethic of Dignity in the Philippines." *PeacePower* 2, no. 1 (Winter): 20–21. www.calpeacepower.org/0201/philippines_people_power.htm.

Scalmer, Sean. 2011. *Gandhi in the West: The Mahatma and the Rise of Radical Protest*. Cambridge: Cambridge University Press.

Schell, Jonathan. 2000. *The Fate of the Earth and the Abolition*. Stanford, CA: Stanford University Press.

Scheuerman, William E. 2022. "'Good-Bye to Nonviolence?'." *Political Research Quarterly* 75, no. 4 (December): 1284–1296. https://doi.org/10.1177/10659129211038611.

Schock, Kurt. 2005. *Unarmed Insurrections: People Power Movements in Nondemocracies*. Minneapolis, MN: University of Minnesota Press.

Shapiro, Judith, and John-Andrew McNeish. 2021. *Our Extractive Age: Expressions of Violence and Resistance*. London: Routledge.

Sharp, Gene. 1960. *Gandhi Wields the Weapon of Moral Power*. Ahmedabad, IN: Navajivan.

Sharp, Gene. 1970. *Exploring Nonviolent Alternatives*. Boston: Porter Sargent.

Sharp, Gene. 1973. *The Politics of Nonviolent Action*. Boston: Porter Sargent.

Sharp, Gene. 2005. *Waging NonViolent Struggle: 20th Century Practice and 21st Century Potential*. Boston, MA: Extending Horizons Books.

Sharp, Gene. 2008. *From Dictatorship to Democracy: A Conceptual Framework for Liberation*. 3rd ed. East Boston, MA: Albert Einstein Institution.

Sheehan, Joanne. 2021. "The Roots of Revolutionary Nonviolence in the United States Are in the Black Community." *War Resisters*, February 15. https://wagingnonviolence.org/wr/2021/02/roots-revolutionary-nonviolence-united-states-are-in-the-black-community/.

Shepard, Mark. 1987. *Gandhi Today: A Report on Mahatma Gandhi's Successors*. Arcata, CA: Simple Productions.

Shiva, Vandana. 2022. *Terra Viva: My Life in a Biodiversity of Movements*. Chelsea: Chelsea Green.

Sibley, Mulford Q. 1963. *The Quiet Battle: Writings on the Theory and Practice of Non-Violent Resistance*. Garden City, NY: Doubleday.

Sibley, Mulford Q. 1967. "Aspects of Nonviolence in American Culture." In *Gandhi: His Relevance for Our Times*, edited by G. Ramachandran and T. K. Mahadevan, 231–245. Berkeley, CA: World without War Council.

Skocpol, Theda, ed. 1984. *Vision and Method in Historical Sociology*. Cambridge: Cambridge University Press.

Smith, Jackie, and Dawn Wiest. 2005. "The Uneven Geography of Global Civil Society: National and Global Influences on Transnational Association." *Social Forces* 84, no. 2 (December): 621–652.

Smith, Marcie. 2019a. "Change Agent: Gene Sharp's Neoliberal Nonviolence (Part One)." *Nonsite.org*, May 10. https://nonsite.org/change-agent-gene-sharps-neoliberal-nonviolence-part-one/.

Smith, Marcie. 2019b. "Getting Gene Sharp Wrong (Part Two)." *Jacobin* https://jacobin.com/2019/12/gene-sharp-george-lakey-neoliberal-nonviolence. Accessed July 6, 2023.

Sombatpoonsiri, Janjira. 2019. *Postprotest Pathways in Thailand: Between the Street and the Ballots*. Washington, DC: Carnegie Endowment for International Peace. https://carnegieeurope.eu/2019/10/24/after-protest-pathways-beyond-mass-mobilization-pub-80135.

Soysal, Yasemin Nuhoğlu. 2012. "Citizenship, Immigration, and the European Social Project: Rights and Obligations of Individuality." *The British Journal of Sociology* 63, no. 1: 1–21. https://doi.org/10.1111/j.1468-4446.2011.01404.x.

Soysal, Yasemin Nuhoglu. 2021a. "Citizenship's Double-Edged Sword: Locating Liberalism and Illiberalism in Citizenship." *International Journal of Constitutional Law* 18, no. 4: 1519–1522. https://doi.org/10.1093/icon/moaa106.

Soysal, Yasemin Nuhoglu. 2021b. "Institutional Underpinnings, Global Reach, and the Future of Ordinal Citizenship." *The British Journal of Sociology* 72, no. 2: 174–180. https://doi.org/10.1111/1468-4446.12837.

Spence, Steve. 2011. "Cultural Globalization and the US Civil Rights Movement." *Public Culture* 23, no. 3 (Fall): 551–572. https://doi.org/10.1215/08992363-1336417.

Spilerman, Seymour. 1970. "The Causes of Racial Disturbances: A Comparison of Alternative Explanations." *American Sociological Review* 35, no. 4 (August): 627–649. https://doi.org/10.2307/2093941.

Springhall, John. 2001. *Decolonization since 1945: The Collapse of European Overseas Empires.* London: Red Globe Press.

Staggenborg, Suzanne. 2013. "Institutionalization of Social Movements." In *The Wiley-Blackwell Encyclopedia of Social and Political Movements*, edited by David A. Snow, Donatella della Porta, Doug McAdam, and Bert Klandermans. London: Blackwell. https://onlinelibrary.wiley.com/doi/10.1002/9780470674871.wbespm113.

Stiehm, Judith. 1968. "Nonviolence Is Two. *Sociological Inquiry* 38, no. 1: 23–30.

Strang, David. 1990. "From Dependency to Sovereignty: An Event History Analysis of Decolonization 1870–1987." *American Sociological Review* 55, no. 6 (December): 846–860. https://doi.org/10.2307/2095750.

Strang, David, and Sarah A. Soule. 1998. "Diffusion in Organizations and Social Movements: From Hybrid Corn to Poison Pills." *Annual Review of Sociology* 24: 265–290. https://doi.org/10.1146/annurev.soc.24.1.265.

Suárez, David, and Patricia Bromley. 2012. "Professionalizing a Global Social Movement: Universities and Human Rights." *American Journal of Education* 118, no. 3 (May): 253–280. https://doi.org/10.1086/664740.

Sutherland, Bill, and Matt Meyer. 2000. *Guns and Gandhi in Africa: Pan-African Insights on Nonviolence, Armed Struggle, and Liberation.* Trenton, NJ: Africa World Press.

Swarthmore College. 2022. "Global Nonviolent Action Database." https://nvdatabase.swarthmore.edu/.

Swerdlow, Amy. 1993. *Women Strike for Peace: Traditional Motherhood and Radical Politics in the 1960s.* Chicago, IL: University of Chicago Press.

Swiss, Liam. 2009. "Decoupling Values from Action: An Event-History Analysis of the Election of Women to Parliament in the Developing World, 1945–90." *International Journal of Comparative Sociology* 50, no. 1: 69–95. https://doi.org/10.1177/0020715208100981.

Szilard, Leo. 1945. "A Petition to the President of the United States." *Atomic Heritage Foundation.* www.atomicheritage.org/key-documents/szilard-petition.

Szmigiera. "Military Spending as GDP Share by Country 2021." *Statista*. December 10, 2022. www.statista.com/statistics/266892/military-expend iture-as-percentage-of-gdp-in-highest-spending-countries/.

Tamayo, Sergio. 1999. *Los Veintes Octubres Mexicanos: La transición a la modernizacion y la democracia, 1968–1988: Ciudadanías e identidades colectivas*. Mexico: Universidad Autónoma Metropolitana-Azcapotzalco.

Tarrow, Sidney. 1998. *Power in Movement: Social Movements and Contentious Politics*, 2nd ed. Cambridge: Cambridge University Press.

Tarrow, Sidney. 2001. "Transnational Politics: Contention and Institutions in International Politics." *Annual Review of Political Science* 4: 1–20. https://doi.org/10.1146/annurev.polisci.4.1.1.

Taylor, Verta, Katrina Kimport, Nella Van Dyke, and Ellen Ann Anderson. 2009. "Culture and Mobilization: Tactical Repertoires, Same-Sex Weddings, and the Impact on Gay Activism." *American Sociological Review* 74, no. 6 (December): 865–890. https://doi.org/10.1177/000312240907400602.

Tilly, Charles. 1993. "Contentious Repertoires in Great Britain, 1758–1834." *Social Science History* 17, no. 2 (Summer): 253–280. https://doi.org/10.2307/1171282.

Tilly, Charles. 1977. "Getting It Together in Burgundy, 1675–1975." *Theory and Society* 4, no. 4 (Winter): 479–504. https://doi.org/10.1007/BF001 87423.

Tilly, Charles. 2004. *Social Movements, 1768–2004*. Boulder, CO: Paradigm.

Tilly, Charles. 2006. *Regimes and Repertoires*. Chicago, IL: University of Chicago Press.

Tilly, Charles. 2008. *Contentious Performances*. Cambridge: Cambridge University Press.

Tilly, Charles, and Sidney Tarrow. 2007. *Contentious Politics*. Boulder, CO: Paradigm.

The Times of India. 1919. "The Satyagraha: Mr. Gandhi Suspends It. Growing Protests against It." April 19. Page 9. ProQuest Historical Newspapers *Times of India* (1838–2002).

Traugott, Mark, ed. 1995. *Repertoires and Cycles of Collective Action*. Durham, NC: Duke University Press.

Tsurumi, Kazuko. 1970. "Some Comments on the Japanese Student Movement in the Sixties." *Journal of Contemporary History* 5, no. 1 (January): 104–112. https://doi.org/10.1177/002200947000500107.

Tsutsui, Kiyoteru. 2017. "Human Rights and Minority Activism in Japan: Transformation of Movement Actorhood and Local-Global Feedback Loop1." *American Journal of Sociology* 122, no. 4 (January): 1050–1103. https://doi.org/10.1086/689910.

Tsutsui, Kiyoteru. 2018. *Rights Make Might Global Human Rights and Minority Social Movements in Japan.* New York: Oxford University Press.

Tsutsui, Kiyoteru, and Hwa Ji Shin. 2008. "Global Norms, Local Activism, and Social Movement Outcomes: Global Human Rights and Resident Koreans in Japan." *Oxford Academic, Social Problems* 55, no. 3 (August): 391–418. https://doi.org/10.1525/sp.2008.55.3.391.

Union of International Associations. 2012. *Union of International Associations.* https://uia.org/yearbook. Accessed July 6, 2023.

UN General Assembly. 1960. *Declaration on the Granting of Independence to Colonial Countries and Peoples.* December 14, UN Doc. A/RES/1514 (XV). www.refworld.org/docid/3b00f06e2f.html. Accessed July 6, 2023.

United Nations. n.d. "Decolonization." Accessed December 10, 2022. www.un.org/en/global-issues/decolonization.

US Department of State. 2018. "Conventional Arms Transfer Policy." www.state.gov/conventional-arms-transfer-cat-policy. Accessed July 6, 2023.

Van den Berk, Jorrit. 2018. "The Promise of Democracy for the Americas: U.S. Diplomacy and the Meanings of World War II in El Salvador, 1941–1945." In *Politics and Cultures of Liberation: Media, Memory, and Projections of Democracy,* edited by Mehring, Frank, Bak, Hans, and Rosa, Mathilde, 241–264. Leiden: The Netherlands.

Wada, Takeshi. 2004. "Event Analysis of Claim Making in Mexico: How are Social Protests Transformed into Political Protests?" *Mobilization: An International Quarterly* 9, no, 3: 241–257. https://doi.org/10.17813/maiq.9.3.7wx2pt66130718v3.

Wada, Takeshi. 2012. "Modularity and Transferability of Repertoires of Contention." *Social Problems* 59, no. 4 (November): 544–571. https://doi.org/10.1525/sp.2012.59.4.544.

Wagner-Pacifici, Robin, and Barry Schwartz. 1991. "The Vietnam Veterans Memorial: Commemorating a Difficult Past." *American Journal of Sociology* 97, no. 2 (September): 276–420. https://doi.org/10.1086/229783.

Walker, Charles. 1967. "The Impact of Gandhi on the U.S. Peace Movement." In *Gandhi: His Relevance for Our Times,* edited by G. Ramachandran and T. K. Mahadevan. Berkeley: World without War Council.

Watanabe, Chika. 2019. *Becoming One: Religion, Development, and Environmentalism in a Japanese NGO in Myanmar.* Honolulu, HI: University of Hawaii Press.

Weber, Thomas. 2004. "The Impact of Gandhi on the Development of Johan Galtung's Peace Research." *Global Change, Peace & Security* 16, no. 1: 31–43. https://doi.org/10.1080/1478115042000176166.

Wiest, Dawn, and Jackie Smith. 2007. "Explaining Participation in Regional Transnational Social Movement Organizations." *International Journal of Comparative Sociology* 48, no. 2–3: 137–166. https://doi.org/10.1177/0020715207075398.

Wittner, Lawrence S. 2009. *Confronting the Bomb: A Short History of the World Nuclear Disarmament Movement*. Stanford, CA: Stanford University Press.

York, Steve, director. 2002. *Bringing Down a Dictator*. York Zimmerman, 56 min.

Zucker, Lynne G. 1987. "Institutional Theories of Organization." *Annual Review of Sociology* 13: 443–464. https://doi.org/10.1146/annurev.so.13.080187.002303.

Zunes, Stephen, Lester R. Kurtz, and Sarah Beth Asher, eds. 1999. *Nonviolent Social Movements: A Geographical Perspective*. Malden, MA: Blackwell.

Zunes, Stephen. 2022. "People-Powered and Non-Violent Social Movements: Forcing Gradualist Democratic Reforms in Authoritarian Societies." *Frontiers in Political Science* 3: 1–15.

Acknowledgements

Just as I was finishing my dissertation research and beginning to give public talks on the globalization of nonviolence, the Middle East erupted in an "Arab Spring." Pundits declared these insurrections a phenomenal historical turning point proving the enduring and growing success of nonviolent civil resistance. Now, as I pen the final pages of this manuscript on that long and winding global history, many of the same scholars are scrambling to explain the disappointing outcomes of those movements and also new waves of authoritarianism and corruption and a deepening fragmentation of long-standing tensions around the world that define the present historical moment. Is nonviolence still the most successful route for civil resistance? Has it always been? These are important questions to ask. For many, they are urgent questions, and I believe careful historical analysis helps to answer them.

As a cultural and political sociologist who thinks about social movements and large-scale political transformations from a global perspective, neither of these recent waves of phenomenal contentious politics has surprised me. I have been thinking carefully about how nonviolence works, how and why it is shared across different movements, how movements engage with nonviolence in common and distinct ways, and why nonviolence fails to achieve the transformations hoped for in certain contexts for over a decade as a scholar and for much longer as a citizen and activist. The work presented here represents a sociological approach to thinking about nonviolence as a global contentious performance, a collective action repertoire that has a particular history, has given life to particular understandings about and engagements with unique political and social issues, and has been shaped by global and transnational forces over the long twentieth and into the early twenty-first century. I have done my best to expand on the work of Charles Tilly by thinking about this unique *global* repertoire as it moves across borders and in drawing on world society research to underscore that those who carry this repertoire across borders, those who work to implement, elaborate, improve upon, and contest it, and the cultural dynamics about how we think about, celebrate, and communicate nonviolence as a best practice for conflict and conflict resolution, all matter in this long and far-reaching history.

Unlike many of the works of the new and developing canon of nonviolent civil resistance studies, my work is neither funded by large nonviolence advocates nor does it set out to prove that nonviolent tactics are superior to violence, however much I personally always root for the path of peace in ends and means.

My work has benefited immensely, however, from the generosity of those who have given their lives to globalizing nonviolence. I am humbled and grateful to have learned from their life stories, their reflections, experiences, and insights.

These illuminating conversations have included interviews with the late Dorothy Cotton, citizenship education coordinator of the Southern Christian Leadership Conference, who worked closely alongside of and wrote a brilliant memoir about Martin Lither King Jr., celebrated and revered leader of the American Civil Rights Movement; the late Lynne Shivers, long-standing organizer with Movement for a New Society and respected author of the movement; and the late Richard Deats, a renowned and beloved peace educator and leader with the International Fellowship for Reconciliation. Richard referred me to Hildegard Goss-Mayr who, along with her late husband Jean, gave the greater part of her life to spreading nonviolence throughout Latin America. I spoke with others in Movement for a New Society, including George Lakey, a celebrated nonviolent strategist, trainer, and author and feminist activist Betsy Raasch-Gilman, whose networks with many other women activists were invaluable in helping me think through feminist responses to and engagements with nonviolence. Many of those women contributed to my anthology *Feminism, Violence and Nonviolence*, forthcoming with Edinburgh University Press.

Enlightening talks were had with Mubarak Awad, Michael Beer, and Matthew Chandler of Nonviolence International who were gracious to allow me to hang around the DC office and who introduced me to many more activists and organizers in the movement. This included Andrei Kemenshikov, regional coordinator for Nonviolence International in the post-Soviet states and Yeshua Moser-Puangsuwan, Nonviolence International coordinator for Southeast Asia.

I had several conversations with activists from Peace Brigades International (PBI), including Executive Director Katherine Hughes-Fraitekh, and I learned much from PBI organizers working in or who had worked in different field sites as well as from the archives of PBI at McMaster University. Several fascinating conversations were had with organizers working in Nonviolent Peaceforce, including David Hartsough and Gilda Bettancourt. I learned much about the daily challenges of supporting NP programs from others in the United States and in Sudan. My conversation with Stephan Van Hook of the Metta Center was very helpful and I appreciated learning from Michael Nagler as well. Maciej Bartkowski, then of International Center for Nonviolent Conflict, shared his insider's perspective on how best to professionalize the spread of nonviolent protest. I learned a great deal from Cora Weiss on her work across decades of anti-war and women's peace movements, from Betty Reardon on the growth of a field for peace education, and from Barbara Wien on her work in conflict zones around the world. Frida Berrigan's reflections on her work against torture were very helpful. Joanne Sheehan has been profoundly generous of her time and knowledge and is someone who I have come to rely on for filling in gaps in my knowledge. She has taught in my classes, connected me with anyone and everyone I have asked her about, and has been an invaluable source of insight and resources to help me better understand the heart of the movement. Pam McAllister's movement histories of women in nonviolence were a breath of fresh air in a dense fog of male battle hero narratives and Pam has also been incredibly generous of her time, reflections, and perspective. I have learned a great deal from many more not listed here but I am appreciative of their knowledge and shared experiences, nonetheless.

Many thanks are due to those who offered comments on early versions of this manuscript at American Sociological Association meetings, the Minority Dissertation Fellowship Program of the ASA, the Tampere University Cultural and Political Sociology colloquium, my former advisors John Boli, Frank Lechner, Alex Hicks, and Ann Hironaka. David Meyer, Suzanne Staggenborg, two anonymous reviewers and everyone who offered assistance at Cambridge University Press, as well as Kim Armstrong for her always helpful edits are all much appreciated.

Finally, I owe my deepest gratitude to the many people whose lives I have pored over and those who shared their lives with me as I have done so, especially Xochitl and Gabriel.

Cambridge Elements ≡

Contentious Politics

David S. Meyer
University of California, Irvine

David S. Meyer is Professor of Sociology and Political Science at the University of California, Irvine. He has written extensively on social movements and public policy, mostly in the United States, and is a winner of the John D. McCarthy Award for Lifetime Achievement in the Scholarship of Social Movements and Collective Behavior.

Suzanne Staggenborg
University of Pittsburgh

Suzanne Staggenborg is Professor of Sociology at the University of Pittsburgh. She has studied organizational and political dynamics in a variety of social movements, including the women's movement and the environmental movement, and is a winner of the John D. McCarthy Award for Lifetime Achievement in the Scholarship of Social Movements and Collective Behavior.

About the Series

Cambridge Elements series in Contentious Politics provides an important opportunity to bridge research and communication about the politics of protest across disciplines and between the academy and a broader public. Our focus is on political engagement, disruption, and collective action that extends beyond the boundaries of conventional institutional politics. Social movements, revolutionary campaigns, organized reform efforts, and more or less spontaneous uprisings are the important and interesting developments that animate contemporary politics; we welcome studies and analyses that promote better understanding and dialogue.

Cambridge Elements ≡

Contentious Politics

Elements in the Series

The Phantom at The Opera: Social Movements and Institutional Politics
Sidney Tarrow

*The Street and the Ballot Box: Interactions Between Social Movements and
Electoral Politics in Authoritarian Contexts*
Lynette H. Ong

Contested Legitimacy in Ferguson: Nine Hours on Canfield Drive
Joshua Bloom

Contentious Politics in Emergency Critical Junctures
Donatella della Porta

Collective Resistance to Neoliberalism
Paul Almeida & Amalia Pérez Martín

Mobilizing for Abortion Rights in Latin America
Mariela Daby and Mason W. Moseley

*Black Networks Matter: The Role of Interracial Contact and Social Media in the 2020
Black Lives Matter Protests*
Matthew David Simonson, Ray Block Jr, James N. Druckman, Katherine
Ognyanova and David M. J. Lazer

Have Repertoire, Will Travel: Nonviolence as Global Contentious Performance
Selina R. Gallo-Cruz

A full series listing is available at: www.cambridge.org/ECTP

Printed in the United States
by Baker & Taylor Publisher Services